Movie Lover's DEVOTIONAL

D0483321

WHAT WE LEARN ABOUT LIFE FROM 60 GREAT HOLLYWOOD FILMS

ED STRAUS AND KEVIN MILLER

BARBOUR
PUBLISHING

ISBN 978-1-60260-748-4

Cover design: Faceout Studio, www.faceoutstudio.com

Published by Barbour Publishing, Inc., P.O. Box 719, Uhrichsville, Ohio 44683 www.barbourbooks.com

Our mission is to publish and distribute inspirational products offering exceptional value and biblical encouragement to the masses.

Member of the
Evangelical Christian
Publishers Association

CONTENTS

 **INTRODUCTION**

If you like movies, you'll love this collection of sixty readings that draw engaging, contemporary spiritual points from film.

From *2001: A Space Odyssey* to *The Wizard of Oz,* from *Ben-Hur* to *WALL-E,* from *Chariots of Fire* to *My Big Fat Greek Wedding,* the films included in this book run the gamut from the 1930s to the present. You'll find comedies and dramas represented, animated features, science-fiction films, Westerns, and more.

Each entry features details on the movie itself, then describes a moment of truth to be found in the film. Though Hollywood isn't always a great friend to the Christian faith, it often poses insightful questions— questions the Bible is ready and willing to tackle.

After each film profile, "Take Two" questions encourage you to think critically about the movie and how its questions relate to your life.

We hope *The Movie Lover's Devotional* will remind you of some great moments in your favorite films. . . introduce you to unfamiliar movies you might want to see. . .and, more importantly, get you thinking about the deeper meanings of both films and life.

*Spoiler Alert: Please note that some readings
may give away key details of these films!*

12 Angry Men

Rated: Unrated

Released April 13, 1957

Written by Reginald Rose

Based on the TV play by Reginald Rose

Directed by Sidney Lumet

Distributed by United Artists

Starring:

Martin Balsam (Juror 1)

John Fiedler (Juror 2)

Lee J. Cobb (Juror 3)

E. G. Marshall (Juror 4)

Jack Klugman (Juror 5)

Ed Binns (Juror 6)

Jack Warden (Juror 7)

Henry Fonda (Juror 8, Mr. Davis)

Joseph Sweeney (Juror 9, Mr. McArdle)

Ed Begley (Juror 10)

George Voskovek (Juror 11)

Robert Webber (Juror 12)

"PREJUDICE ALWAYS
OBSCURES THE TRUTH"

In this dramatic 1957 movie, a twelve-man jury has just heard the closing arguments of a murder case in which a Latino teen from the city slums is accused of stabbing his father to death. The judge then instructs the jurors that they must reach a unanimous verdict—guilty or not guilty—and tells them that a guilty verdict carries a mandatory death sentence.

When the twelve men adjourn to the jury room, they're ready to give a verdict immediately. The evidence seems overwhelming: Two witnesses had testified that they saw and heard the murder, and the teen has a weak alibi. However, juror 8 (Mr. Davis) argues that they owe it to the teen to at least *discuss* the case.

As the jurors reexamine the testimonies and the evidence, juror 9 casts doubt on the testimony of a female eyewitness who may not have been wearing her glasses at the time of the alleged murder; juror 5, who has witnessed actual knife fights, points out the unlikelihood of the teen stabbing his father. Juror 6, who has worked near the noisy crime scene, questions what the witnesses could've actually heard. Mr. Davis also proves the murder weapon is not as unique as the prosecution had claimed.

Very importantly, the deliberations bring out the jurors' prejudices. At first, juror 10 is so bigoted that he votes to have the Hispanic teen executed whether he is guilty or not. Juror 3 is carrying a grudge because his own son struck him, so he believes that *all* teens are capable of killing their parents. As Mr. Davis so aptly points out, "Prejudice always obscures the truth."

This 1957 movie, though a black-and-white drama, is a must-see. It is still relevant because the heart of man is the same today as it was fifty years ago. In fact, people have dealt with these same issues for thousands of years. That's why God had Moses tell the Israelites: "Have nothing to do with a false charge and do not put an innocent or honest person to death" (Exodus 23:7 NIV).

This principle is true whether we're on jury duty or simply making judgment calls in everyday life. We can't afford to judge people's motives and actions according to their superficial appearances or our personal prejudices, but must take the time to examine the issues and the evidence closely.

The first to present his case seems right,
till another comes forward and questions him.
PROVERBS 18:17 NIV

 TAKE TWO

Have you ever found yourself judging someone
before all the "evidence" was in? Did prejudice
enter into your decision? Looking back, what could
you have done differently to give that person a "fair
trial"? What did you learn from that situation?

What can you do today to keep yourself from rash
judgments? Ask God to rein your tongue, as well
as your immediate thoughts, and help you to think
carefully before jumping to conclusions.

I've seen this movie ❏

My Star Review ☆ ☆ ☆ ☆ ☆

2001: a space odyssey

Rated: G

Released April 6, 1968

Written by Stanley Kubrick and Arthur C. Clarke

Based on the story "The Sentinel" by
   Arthur C. Clarke

Directed by Stanley Kubrick

Distributed by Metro-Goldwyn-Mayer

Starring:

Keir Dullea (Dr. David Bowman)

Gary Lockwood (Dr. Frank Poole)

William Sylvester (Dr. Heywood R. Floyd)

Leonard Rossiter (Dr. Andrei Smyslov)

Margaret Tyzack (Elena)

Robert Beatty (Dr. Ralph Halvorsen)

Sean Sullivan (Dr. Bill Michaels)

Douglas Rain (Voice of HAL 9000)

A JOURNEY UNLIKE ANY OTHER

Many of us who saw the 1968 movie *2001: A Space Odyssey* remember stumbling out of the theater afterward, looking at our friends, and asking, "What was that all about?" We had just been taken on a surreal, special-effects journey, felt we had watched something deep and epic, but the enigmatic ending left us hanging.

The movie begins with a group of upright apes in 4 million BC who run across a mysterious black monolith and are transformed into tool-making protohumans. The scene suddenly switches to modern times, and we see that a monolith, like the one that jump-started the apes, has been discovered on the moon.

Eighteen months later, Drs. David Bowman and Frank Poole are en route to Jupiter, though their mission is so secret even they don't know its exact purpose. The ship's computer, "HAL"—which up till now has never erred—begins making mistakes; when the men become suspicious of HAL's motives, HAL kills Frank and tries to kill Dave. Dave survives, however, and shuts HAL down. A video then comes onscreen, revealing that the monolith on the moon had sent a signal to Jupiter.

When Dave approaches a monolith in orbit around Jupiter, he suddenly enters a multicolored "Star Gate," travels through vast reaches of space, and ends up in a room where he sees future visions of himself aging. When he dies, a monolith transforms him into a fetus-like "Star-Child" in an orb of light, who orbits the earth.

Stanley Kubrick intentionally made the film mysterious, but in the book Arthur C. Clarke wrote after the movie was released, Clarke explained the monoliths were tools created by a highly developed alien race that had evolved into a state of pure energy. These aliens traveled the universe, helping lesser species evolve—and apparently their desire was that humankind take the next step beyond mortality to be reborn as higher life forms.

While Christian theology has little room for aliens, there actually are superior beings "out there." They are angels of God—agents of a powerful, all-wise spiritual Being—who are here on Earth to help humans find new life. This new life is called *salvation*, or being "born again" (John 3:3). Like Dave, we must rise above the limits of modern technology if we are to embark on a spiritual journey and discover the deepest mysteries of life.

*Are not all angels ministering spirits sent
to serve those who will inherit salvation?*
HEBREWS 1:14 NIV

 **TAKE TWO**

Do you ever feel you are more plugged in to human technology than to God? What can you do to keep yourself (and your time) from being swallowed up by cell phones, TV, and the Internet?

Each morning, before embarking on your daily life journey, are you establishing contact with the Holy Spirit—our navigational guide—via prayer? If not, what can you do to change that?

I've seen this movie ❏

My Star Review ☆ ☆ ☆ ☆ ☆

AMAZING GRACE

Rated: PG

Released February 23, 2007

Written by Steven Knight

Directed by Michael Apted

Distributed by IDP

Starring:

Ioan Gruffudd (William Wilberforce)

Romola Garai (Barbara Spooner)

Ciarán Hinds (Lord Tarleton)

Rufus Sewell (Thomas Clarkson)

Michael Gambon (Lord Charles Fox)

Albert Finney (John Newton)

Benedict Cumberbatch (William Pitt)

Youssou N'Dour (Olaudah Equiano)

THE POWER TO CHANGE THE WORLD

This docudrama opens in 1797 with British Member of Parliament William Wilberforce taking a holiday at Bath in Somerset. Wilberforce is in failing health and spiritually and mentally drained. When he meets beautiful young Barbara Spooner, Wilberforce begins sharing his frustrations and sorrows.

Spooner learns that fifteen years earlier, Wilberforce had entered politics as an ambitious, idealistic, and popular young man. After he became a Christian, however, he had been influenced by Thomas Clarkson and a group of believers dedicated to the abolition of slavery.

With a handful of staunch allies, including John Newton—a former slave ship captain who wrote the hymn "Amazing Grace"—Prime Minister William Pitt, and Olaudah Equiano, a former slave, Wilberforce had labored tirelessly to try to pass antislavery legislation, only to run into public apathy and strong opposition from politicians led by Lord Tarleton, who defended the lucrative slave trade.

After fifteen years of fruitless fighting—and merely succeeding in becoming highly unpopular—Wilberforce was exhausted and wanted to give up politics. Spooner, however, persuades him to keep fighting, saying that if he doesn't champion this cause, no one will. The two are caught up in a whirlwind romance and soon marry. Encouraged, Wilberforce presses on and eventually, after a prolonged fight, succeeds: The slave trade is banished throughout the British Empire.

The movie shows the power of the gospel: The words of Christ have not only the power to bring us into a personal relationship with God, but the power to help us to live out the gospel—and that often means, like Wilberforce, becoming involved with worthy causes to help others. (See Proverbs 23:11–12.)

This movie is also a testament to the empire-shaking power of a handful of people persevering against all odds for the sake of a just cause. It is a tribute to the power of encouragement and unflinching friendship. God might call you to be like Wilberforce and stand up for what's right, or to be like Spooner and encourage those who are taking such a stand. Whichever you are called to be, fight the good fight and don't give up!

Let us not become weary in doing good,
for at the proper time we will reap
a harvest if we do not give up.
GALATIANS 6:9 NIV

 TAKE TWO

Is God calling you to take a stand either for someone weaker than yourself or for a just cause? Pray for the courage to do so. And once you've taken that first step, don't give up, no matter how great the odds!

Do you have a friend who needs someone to spur them on? Ask God who needs your encouragement today; then give it!

I've seen this movie ❑

My Star Review ☆ ☆ ☆ ☆ ☆

ANACONDAS
THE HUNT FOR THE BLOOD ORCHID

Rated: PG-13

Released August 27, 2004

Written by John Claflin, Daniel Zelman, Edward Neumeier, and Michael Miner

Based on a story by Jim Cash, Jack Epps Jr., and Hans Bauer

Directed by Dwight H. Little

Distributed by Screen Gems

Starring:

Johnny Messner (Bill Johnson)

KaDee Strickland (Samantha "Sam" Rogers)

Matthew Marsden (Dr. Jack Byron)

Nicholas Gonzalez (Dr. Ben Douglas)

Eugene Byrd (Cole Burris)

Karl Yune (Tran)

Salli Richardson (Gail Stern)

Morris Chestnut (Gordon Mitchell)

SEEKING IMMORTALITY

This movie hasn't always received the best reviews, yet its fans strongly defend both the quality of its plot and its acting. The main criticism against it is that it calls the monstrous snakes of Borneo "anacondas" (which are native to South America) rather than pythons—but if you can get past that detail, the movie delivers nonstop entertainment and an even better message.

A greedy pharmaceutical company has discovered the extremely rare blood orchid along a remote river in Borneo, and since its serum reputedly contains the secret to indefinitely prolonging life, it sends a scientific expedition, led by Dr. Jack Byron, to harvest the blooms. The profits from marketing an "immortality drug" would be astronomical, and this brings out the very worst in the ruthless Dr. Byron.

It's the beginning of the dangerous rainy season, and only Captain Bill Johnson is willing to take them upriver on his boat. As tension builds and one thrill and spill follows another, the expedition learns that the blood orchid is part of the diet of the local anacondas (pythons). These snakes continue to grow as long as they live and have thus reached gargantuan sizes. They now begin devouring the expedition members one by one.

The survivors finally reach the place where the blood orchid grows, and see that it's above a pit where the giant snakes have gathered to mate. In the action-packed climax, Dr. Byron threatens to kill all who stand in his way, but instead, he is eaten alive by a serpent. Another attacking python bites into a fuel can, is shot with a flare gun, then explodes in a fireball that destroys the pit full of serpents and, presumably, the blood orchids.

Adam and Eve were driven out of the garden of Eden because their souls had been corrupted by evil and God said that unregenerate man "must not be allowed to reach out his hand and take also from the tree of life and eat, and live forever" (Genesis 3:22 NIV). This movie demonstrates clearly why wicked, greedy humankind cannot be permitted to barge back into Eden and seize immortality.

Eternal life is to be found not through blood orchids, but by accepting the blood of Christ as payment for our sins (see 1 Peter 1:18–19; Revelation 5:9) and receiving Christ as Lord.

*To those who by persistence in doing good seek glory,
honor and immortality, he will give eternal life.*
ROMANS 2:7 NIV

■ TAKE TWO

God's greatest gift is eternal life. Have you helped
someone else find it in Jesus Christ? Ask God to put
a pre-Christian's name on your heart, one whom you
can help find the Way to eternity.

Instead of worrying about or running after material
things, we are to "seek first [God's] kingdom and
his righteousness" (Matthew 6:33 NIV) and He will
provide everything else. What are you seeking today?
Is God your first priority?

I've seen this movie ❑

My Star Review ☆ ☆ ☆ ☆ ☆

APOLLO 13

Rated: PG

Released June 30, 1995

Written by William Broyles Jr. and Al Reinert

Based on the book *Lost Moon* by Jim Lovell
  and Jeffrey Kluger

Directed by Ron Howard

Distributed by Universal Pictures

Starring:

Tom Hanks (Astronaut Jim Lovell)

Bill Paxton (Astronaut Fred Haise)

Kevin Bacon (Astronaut Jack Swigert)

Gary Sinise (Astronaut Ken Mattingly)

Ed Harris (Flight Director Gene Kranz)

Kathleen Quinlan (Marilyn Lovell)

Tracy Reiner (Mary Haise)

"LET'S WORK THE PROBLEM, PEOPLE"

So many things went wrong with the Apollo 13 moon mission that it seemed jinxed. Four days before launch, a reporter asked astronauts Lovell, Haise, and Mattingly if the number 13 bothered them: "Apollo 13, lifting off at 1300 hours and 13 minutes and entering the moon's gravity on April 13th?"

The astronauts knew that a lot could potentially go wrong, though not due to "bad luck." But they also knew they were well-trained and had a dedicated, professional team behind them.

Two days before the launch, Mattingly, having been exposed to the measles, is replaced by Jack Swigert. After liftoff, trouble begins when Swigert does a routine stir of the oxygen tanks, causing an explosion in the command module *Odyssey*. Mission control cancels the moon landing and orders all three astronauts to move into the *Aquarius*, the two-man Lunar Excursion Module (LEM). They must get back to Earth before their oxygen runs out, and to save energy they shut down the power and huddle in the cold.

Seeking solutions in how to get the astronauts back, Flight Director Gene Kranz tells the men of mission control: "Failure is not an option. . . . Let's work the problem, people."

Later Houston realizes the *Aquarius* wasn't built to filter out all the carbon dioxide created by three men. An engineering team is assembled in Houston, a replicate of every available part the astronauts can cannibalize is dumped on a table, and the engineers are told that's all they have to work with. Their invention is crude, but following their instructions, the astronauts put together an air filter made of, among other things, duct tape, a sock, and the flight-plan cover.

After the climactic reentry into the earth's atmosphere, the astronauts splash down safely, thanks to their courage and training and the ingenuity of their ground crew. Working together, they transformed a bleak, "jinxed" moon mission into a victory over every problem encountered.

The Bible speaks a great deal about the importance of sticking together and using new methods to overcome opposition. Nehemiah and his men, while rebuilding the walls of Jerusalem, were forced to improvise again and again to meet challenges (see Nehemiah 4:7–23). Like them, we must work together and face problems with both courage and ingenuity.

*Two are better than one, because they have a good
return for their work: If one falls down,
his friend can help him up.*
ECCLESIASTES 4:9–10 NIV

🎬 TAKE TWO

Have you ever been up against a problem amid
seemingly insurmountable odds? Did you have the
mind-set that "failure is not an option"? If you had,
would the end result have been different?

Are you currently in a tough situation? Perhaps a
friend (or a team of people) can give you either a
new way of thinking or help you work through the
problem.

I've seen this movie ❏

My Star Review ☆ ☆ ☆ ☆ ☆

BACK TO THE FUTURE

Rated: PG

Released July 3, 1985

Written by Robert Zemeckis and Bob Gale

Directed by Robert Zemeckis

Distributed by Universal Pictures

Starring:

Michael J. Fox (Marty McFly)

Christopher Lloyd (Dr. Emmett Brown)

Lea Thompson (Lorraine Baines McFly)

Crispin Glover (George McFly)

Thomas F. Wilson (Biff Tannen)

Claudia Wells (Jennifer Parker)

James Tolkan (Mr. Strickland)

Huey Lewis (School Band Audition Judge)

DON'T LOOK BACK

The 1985 fantasy *Back to the Future* is just one in a long string of time-travel movies. But its clever take on tampering with history makes it one of the most enjoyable.

Teen skateboarder Marty McFly ("a slacker," according to his high school principal, Mr. Strickland) hangs out with Hill Valley's eccentric inventor, Dr. Emmett Brown. Early one morning, in the parking lot of the local mall, Marty is videotaping Doc's latest experiment when trouble arrives in the form of Libyan terrorists. It seems Brown cheated the bad guys out of a chest full of plutonium to power his invention—a time machine built into a DeLorean sports car. As the Libyans catch up to Doc to exact their revenge, Marty jumps into the car to escape their wrath—and finds himself shot thirty years back in time, to November 5, 1955. Brown had punched that date into the time machine's keypad as the day he'd discovered time travel. More importantly, it was shortly before Marty's parents, George McFly and Lorraine Baines, fell in love.

Marty's unexpected appearance in history, of course, causes a number of comical problems, the biggest being his disruption of George and Lorraine's courtship. With the help of a thirty-years-younger Doc Brown, Marty schemes to bring George and Lorraine back together and ensure his own future existence. To call the balance of the film a roller-coaster ride would be an understatement—but, not surprisingly, the story ends happily.

Fans of the film can probably quote Doc's pronouncement that the "flux capacitor"—a y-shaped glass tube pulsating with light waves—is "what makes time travel possible." We love to imagine the possibilities of time travel—though in reality we're all time travelers. We just move in a single direction at a common speed.

Every individual is moving forward in time, second by second, minute by minute, day by day. Living in the past is great for the movies, but not an option in real life. That's why the apostle Paul kept a sharp focus on the end of his life journey: "One thing I do: Forgetting what is behind and straining toward what is ahead, I press on toward the goal to win the prize for which God has called me heavenward in Christ Jesus (Philippians 3:13–14 NIV).

We really don't have time to dwell on the past.

*Jesus replied, "No one who puts his hand
to the plow and looks back is fit for service
in the kingdom of God."*
LUKE 9:62 NIV

🎬 TAKE TWO

Do you find yourself dwelling on things you
should've, could've, would've done? Is that keeping
you from moving forward? If so, ask God to give you
peace about yesterday and vision for today.

Look forward by setting some goals for your life.
Where do you see yourself one, five, ten years from
now? Ask God to plant a goal in your heart—then
start traveling in that direction!

I've seen this movie ❑

My Star Review ☆ ☆ ☆ ☆ ☆

A BEAUTIFUL MIND

Rated: PG-13

Released January 4, 2002

Written by Akiva Goldsman

Based on the book by Sylvia Nasar

Directed by Ron Howard

Distributed by Universal Studios / DreamWorks

Starring:

Russell Crowe (John Nash)

Ed Harris (Parcher)

Jennifer Connelly (Alicia Nash)

Christopher Plummer (Dr. Rosen)

Paul Bettany (Charles)

Adam Goldberg (Sol)

Josh Lucas (Hansen)

Anthony Rapp (Bender)

THE COURAGE OF THE HEART

A *Beautiful Mind* recalls the life of Nobel Prize–winning economist and mathematician John Forbes Nash whose ability to see patterns where no one else does leads to brilliant discoveries in governing dynamics and game theory. But it also entangles him in paranoid delusions that ultimately impact his relationships, health, and work. We see him descend into a self-made world where he works for the Department of Defense, decoding Soviet Cold War encryptions supposedly hidden in newspapers and magazines. His mental illness also threatens his wife and child. How Nash faces this dilemma carries us through to the final scene of the film, when he receives his Nobel Prize.

At a key point in the film, Nash is desperately in search of an original idea for his graduate research project. Then one night he has an epiphany while hanging out with some friends in a pub. A beautiful woman enters the bar with an entourage of friends, catching everyone's attention. Nash realizes that if he and his friends all compete to pursue her, she will reject them all, and her friends will not consent to playing second fiddle. Nobody wins. The best response is to break the impasse by cooperating for a solution in which everyone wins—in this case, by agreeing to set aside their first preference and for each one to approach one of the other girls.

Nash's "Aha!" moment has been practically applied in politics and business to analyze the way decision-makers interact. In our world of tit-for-tat, individuals, groups, and nations become so stuck in their own interests, their need to get ahead, or their obsession to defeat their enemies that everyone loses. Someone needs to risk thinking outside the box so the cycle of human self-destruction can be broken. Such wisdom is all too rare but not at all hard to find. We can read about it in Jesus' Sermon on the Mount (see Matthew 5–7).

Jesus taught radical principles for overcoming evil with good, ending violence with peace, and defeating greed with generosity. He was the all-time expert on creatively applying love as the grand solution to hatred. But He not only taught us how to be "good Christians"—He showed us how to be better humans with courageous hearts.

Jesus was prepared to lose that others might win, demonstrating this most clearly in His death on the cross. Rather than responding in wrath, He forgave, reconciling us to God. This was the beautiful mind *and* beautiful heart of Jesus.

Whoever finds his life will lose it,
and whoever loses his life for my sake will find it.
MATTHEW 10:39 NIV

 **TAKE TWO**

Think back to a time when you were involved in
a lose-lose situation. How could you have applied
Christ's principles to create a different outcome?

Are you "caught in the cycle" of sin right now—
either your own sin or someone else's? How can you
apply Christ's "out of the box" thinking to help you
break free?

I've seen this movie ❏

My Star Review ☆ ☆ ☆ ☆ ☆

BEN-HUR

Rated: G

Released November 18, 1959

Written by Karl Tunberg, Gore Vidal (uncredited),
   and Christopher Fry (uncredited)

Based on the novel by Lew Wallace

Directed by William Wyler

Distributed by Metro-Goldwyn-Mayer

Starring:

Charlton Heston (Judah Ben-Hur)

Stephen Boyd (Messala)

Martha Scott (Miriam)

Cathy O'Donnell (Tirzah)

Haya Harareet (Esther)

Sam Jaffe (Simonides)

Jack Hawkins (Quintus Arrius)

Hugh Griffith (Sheik Ilderim)

Finlay Currie (Balthasar)

Frank Thring (Pontius Pilate)

A SWORD IN HAND

This classic film tells the story of Judah Ben-Hur, a rich Jewish merchant living in Jerusalem with his mother, Miriam, and sister, Tirzah. His childhood friend, a Roman named Messala, has returned to Jerusalem as commanding officer of the Jerusalem garrison, prepared to quell potential uprisings. Messala, committed to the Roman vision of ruling with military might, becomes angry when Ben-Hur refuses to betray his people as an informer.

When a tile falls off the Ben-Hur roof, causing the new governor's horse to throw and nearly injure him, Messala decides to make an example out of his former friends—even though he knows it was an accident: He sends Miriam and Tirzah to prison and condemns Judah Ben-Hur to spend the rest of his life as a galley slave. Marched off in chains, Ben-Hur swears revenge.

As Ben-Hur rows, now a mere number, the Roman consul, Quintus Arrius, says to him, "Your eyes are full of hate, forty-one. That's good. Hate keeps a man alive. It gives him strength." Arrius takes a liking to Ben-Hur and leaves him unchained, so when their ship sinks, Ben-Hur in turn rescues Arrius. In gratitude, Arrius legally adopts Ben-Hur, conferring on him riches and power, and Ben-Hur becomes a professional charioteer.

Driven by a thirst for revenge, Ben-Hur returns to Jerusalem where he is told his mother and sister died in prison. Learning that there will be chariot races and Messala is the current champion, Ben-Hur enters the race and wins—while Messala is trampled by horses. But even this victory doesn't bring peace to Ben-Hur.

Ben-Hur learns that his mother and sister are not dead but are lepers, living in a leper colony, but as Jesus dies on the cross they are miraculously healed. After Ben-Hur hears Jesus say, "Father, forgive them, for they know not what they do," he says, "I felt His voice take the sword out of my hand."

Like Ben-Hur, many of us today need to allow Jesus to take the swords out of our hands. We need to let go of grudges. Yes, others have wronged us and hurt us, but if we are to find peace, we must forgive them, forsake revenge, and allow God to make things right.

Do not repay anyone evil for evil. . . .
Do not take revenge. . .for it is written:
"It is mine to avenge; I will repay," says the Lord.
ROMANS 12:17, 19 NIV

TAKE TWO

It has been said that nursing unforgiveness is like taking poison in hopes that your enemy will die. Are you poisoned with bitterness? Take the remedy: Go to Jesus in prayer, asking Him to cleanse your mind and give you the power to forgive.

Can you think back to a time when you wronged someone else—either intentionally or unintentionally? If so, do that person and yourself a favor. Ask him or her for forgiveness. In doing so, you will find the peace that surpasses all understanding.

I've seen this movie ❑

My Star Review ☆ ☆ ☆ ☆ ☆

BRAVEHEART

Rated: R

Released May 24, 1995

Written by Randall Wallace

Directed by Mel Gibson

Distributed by Paramount Pictures

Starring:

Mel Gibson (William Wallace)

Catherine McCormack (Murron MacClannough)

Sophie Marceau (Princess Isabelle)

Patrick McGoohan (King Edward I, Longshanks)

Ian Bannen (The Leper, Robert the Bruce Sr.)

Angus Macfadyen (Robert the Bruce)

Brendan Gleeson (Hamish Campbell)

Brian Cox (Argyle Wallace)

STANDING UP FOR FREEDOM

When Scotland was in a divided state, King Edward I of England invaded and occupied the land. He pacified the Scottish rulers, such as Robert the Bruce Sr., who then did nothing while the English nobles oppressed the common people. These English nobles also received the scandalous privilege of *Primae Noctis* (First Night), which gave them the "right" to spend the wedding night with all new Scottish brides.

When William Wallace, son of a murdered Scottish noble, falls in love with lovely Murron MacClannough, they marry secretly to avoid her being violated. The local English lord finds out, however, and has the sheriff publicly execute her. William is so enraged that he leads the villagers to wipe out the entire garrison and burn down the castle. Then all Scotland rises behind him in open revolt.

William defeats the English in a series of stunning battles, but Scottish nobles, not wishing to lose their comfort and social standing, refuse to join him. Two nobles betray William, and later Robert the Bruce Sr., heir to the Scottish throne, captures William and hands him over to the English. William is tortured but refuses to give up his convictions. He dies with the shout of "Freedom!" It is left to Robert the Bruce's idealist son to pick up William's fight and drive the English out.

In the Bible, the weak, divided Israelites were frequently conquered by foreign invaders, who then occupied their land and oppressed them. God repeatedly raised up courageous leaders who rallied the people to drive them out. Examples of such men are Othniel, Ehud, Barak, Gideon, and Jephthah, but Barak fits the example of *Braveheart* closest, for although tribes like Issachar followed Barak and "the people of Zebulun risked their very lives" (Judges 5:18 NIV), many Israelite tribes—Gilead, Dan, and Asher—like the Scottish nobility, stayed home and refused to fight (see Judges chapters 4–5).

God is still looking for brave men and women today who will say "Enough!" and rise up and set a godly example for others to follow. And when the call goes forth to rise up, make a difference, and change things that need to be changed, we need to be ready to stand with God's people.

*"For the leaders who took the lead in Israel,
for the people who offered themselves willingly,
bless the Lord!"*
JUDGES 5:2 AMP

 **TAKE TWO**

Is there a time in your past when you wish you would
have risen up to meet a challenge, but didn't? What
did you learn from that situation?

Do you currently have a call to rise up and make a
difference? Do you have the courage to do so? If not,
ask God to fill you with strength and wisdom, then
step out in faith, knowing He'll be with you as you
stand amid His people.

I've seen this movie ❏

My Star Review ☆ ☆ ☆ ☆ ☆

Casablanca

Rated: PG

Released January 23, 1943

Written by Julius J. Epstein, Philip G. Epstein,
  Howard Koch, and Casey Robinson (uncredited)

Based on the play *Everybody Comes to Rick's* by
  Murray Burnett and Joan Alison

Directed by Michael Curtiz

Distributed by Warner Bros.

Starring:

Humphrey Bogart (Rick Blaine)

Ingrid Bergman (Ilsa Lund)

Paul Henreid (Victor Laszlo)

Claude Rains (Captain Renault)

Conrad Veidt (Major Strasser)

Sydney Greenstreet (Signor Ferrari)

Peter Lorre (Ugarte)

Dooley Wilson (Sam)

"HERE'S LOOKING AT YOU, KID"

Casablanca endures among Hollywood's top ro-mantic dramas of all time, its stars delivering some of cinema's quintessential performances in this war-time story of intrigue, sacrifice, and love.

Set in Casablanca under Nazi occupation of Vichy-controlled Morocco, the movie takes place primarily in Rick's Café Américain, a nightclub where all the city's dodgy "players" convene to gamble and connive. The story revolves around Rick Blaine's tense reunion with an ex-lover (Ilsa) and her fugitive husband, Victor Laszlo, and Rick's possession of two letters of transit—hot items for those who would escape the Nazi dragnet. Questions of honor and sacrifice soon arise: Will Rick sell the letters to the highest bidder, withholding them from the couple out of resentment? Will Ilsa take them at gunpoint so she and her husband can escape? Will Rick use the letters to steal off with Ilsa himself? The movie climaxes in a double- then triple-cross that leads to a bittersweet ending and the famous line, "Louis, I think this is the beginning of a beautiful friendship."

As the story progresses, Rick and Ilsa reconcile, yet must battle through their unresolved feelings and implications of her marriage. Their struggle is expressed in the lyrics of the film's famous musical piece, "As Time Goes By," the love song that piano-player Sam is asked to play "for old times' sake."

> It's still the same old story,
> A fight for love and glory,
> A case of do or die.

The characters, compromised by feigned neutrality (Rick), opportunism (Louis), crime (Ugarte), or love (Ilsa), must rise to make difficult and transforming decisions after which they are no longer the same. The active ingredient that determines the quality of their choices and character is whether they will continue to serve self, others, or some higher good.

God allows us to experience circumstances that test and develop our character. Instead of rescuing us from fiery trials, He calls us to pass through them with a view to purging pride and arrogance, and fashioning us into the image of Jesus. Love and glory come not by power and privilege but through "taking up your cross" and following Jesus.

Christ's death did not exempt us from following in His footsteps. We will find that, when the dust of our earthly lives has settled, the final sum is a series of do-or-die scenarios that led us into "a beautiful friend-ship" with God.

[Jesus said] "If anyone would come after me,
he must deny himself and take up his cross and
follow me. For whoever wants to save his life
will lose it, but whoever loses his life for me
and for the gospel will save it."
Mark 8:34–35 NIV

▄▄ TAKE TWO

Crucible experiences often reveal our true character. When was the last time you faced a difficult decision? What did you learn about yourself as a result?

God often allows us to experience trials in order to help us grow and learn. What might God be trying to teach you through the issues you're struggling with right now?

I've seen this movie ❏

My Star Review ☆ ☆ ☆ ☆ ☆

CHARIOTS OF FIRE

Rated: PG	
Released October 9, 1981	
Written by Colin Welland	
Directed by Hugh Hudson	
Distributed by Warner Bros.	

Starring:

Ben Cross (Harold Abrahams)

Ian Charleson (Eric Liddell)

Nicholas Farrell (Aubrey Montague)

Nigel Havers (Lord Andrew Lindsay)

Cheryl Campbell (Jennie Liddell)

Alice Krige (Sybil Gordon, Abrahams's wife)

Lindsay Anderson (Hugh Kerr Anderson, Master of Caius)

Sir John Gielgud (J. J. Thomson, Master of Trinity)

Sir Ian Holm (Sam Mussabini, Abrahams's coach)

"HOPE IN OUR HEARTS
AND WINGS ON OUR HEELS"

This dramatic sports movie is based upon the true story of two British athletes, Eric Liddell and Harold Abrahams, training for and competing in the 1924 Summer Olympics in Paris, France. Harold is a Jewish student in Cambridge University who must overcome anti-Semitism in order to achieve the honor of representing the university in the 100–meter race.

Eric and his sister Jenny are preparing to go to China as missionaries, but in the meantime, Eric sees running as a way to bring glory to God. Jenny tells him that she's concerned that he's getting sidetracked from their goal; Eric answers that he still intends to become a missionary. "I believe God made me for a purpose, but He also made me fast. And when I run, I feel His pleasure."

Harold watches as Eric runs in a race, is tripped, and falls—but gets up again, makes up for the loss, and wins the race. "He runs like an *animal*!" Harold exclaims. Later, using the publicity of his win as a plat-

49

form, Eric preaches a sermon using the text of Isaiah 40:31, comparing life to a race.

On the boat to France, Eric learns that the qualifying heats will be run on a Sunday, and his convictions forbid him to run on the day of rest. The British Olympic committee, together with the Prince of Wales, pressures him to compromise, but Eric stands firm. Then a teammate, Lord Andrew Lindsey, trades places with Eric. Andrew will run the 100 meters on Sunday, and Eric can take Andrew's place in the 400-meter race on Tuesday. Eric runs and wins.

Whether or not you think running on Sunday is a sin, you have to admire the fact that Eric risked losing all he had worked so hard for for the sake of his convictions. And the truth is, we are often tested to see whether we will compromise on issues of faith, both large and small. The question is: Will we stay true to our convictions?

In Hebrews 12:1, we are told that we need to "run with perseverance the race marked out for us"—in other words, stay within the marked-out lines; don't run out of bounds or break God's rules.

*Do you not know that in a race all the runners run,
but only one gets the prize? Run in such a way
as to get the prize.*
1 CORINTHIANS 9:24 NIV

 **TAKE TWO**

Have you compromised your faith after bowing under pressure? What did you learn from that experience? Is it one you would want to repeat?

Isaiah 40:31 says that those who wait upon the Lord will renew their strength. Are you being challenged today in the area of your faith? If so, wait on and put your hope in the Lord. He'll give you the strength to carry you through any- and everything.

I've seen this movie ❏

My Star Review ☆ ☆ ☆ ☆ ☆

Charlie
AND THE
CHOCOLATE
FACTORY

Rated: PG

Released July 15, 2005

Written by John August

Based on the novel by Roald Dahl

Directed by Tim Burton

Distributed by Warner Bros.

Starring:

Johnny Depp (Willy Wonka)

Freddie Highmore (Charlie Bucket)

David Kelly (Grandpa Joe)

Helena Bonham Carter (Mrs. Bucket)

Missi Pyle (Mrs. Beauregarde)

James Fox (Mr. Salt)

Christopher Lee (Dr. Wonka)

"THE BEST KIND OF PRIZE"

Charlie Bucket lives a destitute life in London. Crammed into a tiny shack with his parents and bedridden grandparents, Charlie is reminded of his family's sorry financial state each day as he walks past Willy Wonka's chocolate factory.

Then one day Wonka announces a contest that will allow five lucky children to tour his factory. All they have to do is find one of the golden tickets hidden inside five chocolate bars. Mayhem ensues as children all over the world scramble to find the lucky tickets.

One day Charlie finds some money in the street. Desperately hungry, he buys two chocolate bars. Lo and behold, inside the second bar is the final golden ticket! So Charlie and his Grandpa Joe join the other four winners for the tour of a lifetime. Best of all, Wonka promises that at the end of the tour, one child will receive a prize far greater than they can imagine. But things aren't at all as Charlie expected: The other four children are insufferable brats, and Willy Wonka is the strangest man Charlie has ever met. Nevertheless, he is enraptured by Wonka and his incredible factory. As the tour progresses though, one by one the other children fall victim to their vices—greed, anger, selfishness, and gluttony. In the end, only Charlie remains and wins the prize—the factory itself!

But with one stipulation: Charlie must say good-bye to his family forever. When Charlie refuses, Wonka is stunned. Only when Charlie helps Wonka reunite with his own father does he finally understand Charlie's choice and the importance of family. So he invites Charlie *and* his family to live with him in the factory.

Coming from a humble background, unremarkable in his appearance, and seemingly without any special abilities, Charlie is an unlikely hero. But he has one thing the rest of the children lack: character, reminding us of Christ's words in Matthew 7:13–14: "Wide is the gate and broad is the road that leads to destruction, and many enter through it. But small is the gate and narrow the road that leads to life, and only a few find it" (NIV). Charlie found the narrow gate, and that proved him worthy to win the factory.

What about us? Are we going to exchange our inheritance for a "mess of pottage" (see Genesis 25:29–34), or are we willing to hold out for the ultimate prize?

*Do you not know that in a race all the runners run,
but only one gets the prize? Run in such a way
as to get the prize.*
1 Corinthians 9:24 NIV

TAKE TWO

Have you been tempted to compromise your principles
in certain areas lately, instead of holding out for all
that God has for you? Ask God to help you resist
temptation so you can remain faithful to the end.

Many people live lives of quiet desperation, hoping to
find a "golden ticket" one day. If this describes you,
how might you find contentment in the here and
now despite your circumstances?

I've seen this movie ❑

My Star Review ☆ ☆ ☆ ☆ ☆

THE CHRONICLES OF
NARNIA
PRINCE CASPIAN

Rated: PG

Released May 16, 2008

Written by Andrew Adamson, Christopher Markus, and Stephen McFeely

Based upon the novel by C. S. Lewis

Directed by Andrew Adamson

Distributed by Walt Disney Pictures

Starring:

Ben Barnes (Prince Caspian)

William Moseley (Peter Pevensie)

Anna Popplewell (Susan Pevensie)

Skandar Keynes (Edmund Pevensie)

Georgie Henley (Lucy Pevensie)

Sergio Castellitto (King Miraz)

Damián Alcázar (Lord Sopespian)

Peter Dinklage (Trumpkin)

Liam Neeson (Voice of Aslan)

FROM HAUGHTY TO HUMBLE

The four Pevensie children—Peter, Susan, Edmund, and Lucy—have been back in England for one year when suddenly, while waiting on an underground rail platform, they are transported back to Narnia. Some thirteen hundred years have passed there, however, and the Telmarines have invaded, killing the Narnians and driving the survivors into the forest. When evil King Miraz seeks to kill Prince Caspian, the rightful heir to the Telmarine throne, Caspian escapes into the forest. Pursued by Miraz's men, in mortal danger, he blows a legendary horn, which summons the Pevensies.

By the time Peter and his siblings arrive, led by Trumpkin the dwarf, Prince Caspian has rallied the Narnians and persuaded them to battle his uncle. Peter had once ruled Narnia as High King and expects to be honored as such again, but Caspian is now heir apparent and is unwilling to step aside. The two young men find themselves in a struggle for leadership.

Peter suggests launching an attack against Miraz's

castle, and though Caspian argues against it he's over-ruled. When the attack fails, many Narnians are killed and the rest retreat in defeat to Aslan's How. Peter and Caspian blame each other for the failure of the mission and Peter pointedly reminds Caspian, "*You* called us! Remember?" "My first mistake," Caspian retorts. "No," Peter replies. "Your first mistake was thinking you could lead these people."

In the end, the two agree on a united plan to defend the stronghold of Aslan's How, and use both their strengths to fight the attacking Telmarines. Even that is not enough, however, and they are in danger of being overrun when Lucy reaches Aslan, who returns and calls the dryads (tree-beings) and the river god to help. Narnia is saved, the Pervensies return to Earth, and Caspian remains to rule Narnia.

Commenting about this power struggle, actor William Moseley said, "It's a lot about humility. I think they both have to learn a certain humility. . .and that's really what a great king needs is to be humble." This is true. Power struggles, jealousy, and bickering are all too common, even among Christians. That's why Paul advised Christians, "Submit to one another out of reverence for Christ" (Ephesians 5:21 NIV).

*Do nothing out of selfish ambition or vain conceit,
but in humility consider others better than yourselves.*
PHILIPPIANS 2:3 NIV

 **TAKE TWO**

Have you ever found yourself unwilling to
compromise, resulting in friction instead of harmony?
What progress was made as a result of contention?

Jesus said that whoever humbles himself will be
exalted and vice versa (see Matthew 23:12). Would
knowing this seemingly paradoxical maxim make you
more willing to bow to others?

I've seen this movie ❏

My Star Review ☆ ☆ ☆ ☆ ☆

CLOSE ENCOUNTERS
OF THE THIRD KIND

Rated: PG

Released November 16, 1977

Written by Steven Spielberg

Based on the book *The UFO Experience* by
   Dr. J. Allen Hynek

Directed by Steven Spielberg

Distributed by Columbia Studios

Starring:

Richard Dreyfuss (Roy Neary)

Teri Garr (Ronnie Neary)

Shawn Bishop (Brad Neary)

Adrienne Campbell (Sylvia Neary)

Justin Dreyfuss (Toby Neary)

Melinda Dillon (Jillian Guiler)

Bob Balaban (David Laughlin)

François Truffaut (Claude Lacombe)

J. Patrick McNamara (Project Leader)

Warren J. Kemmerling (Wild Bill)

DRIVEN TRUTH-SEEKERS, PRESS ON!

When Steven Spielberg created *Close Encounters of the Third Kind* in the late seventies, it was a welcome relief from the many "evil alien" movies that had preceded and later succeeded it.

The movie opens with numerous incidents of close encounters of the *first* kind—sightings. (Close encounters of the *second* kind are physical effects.) When Roy Neary, an electrical lineman, is sent out to fix a power outage, he sees a UFO above him and a mental image of a mountain is implanted in his mind. Neary becomes obsessed with making replicas of this mountain, so much so that his family thinks he's gone crazy.

When Neary sees news about a train wreck near Devil's Tower National Monument in Wyoming, he realizes that is "it," forsakes everything, and sets out. The US Army has cordoned off the area, however, saying that poisonous gas is leaking, and soon begins hunting down those who have witnessed UFOs. Along the way, Neary meets a single mother, Jillian Guiler, who, like Neary and several other "chosen ones," feels compelled to head to the butte.

Only Neary and Guiler make it to the top, however. There they see why the military is trying to keep the public and truth-seekers away: It wants to maintain tight control over any close encounters of the *third* kind (contact with aliens). The military has built a landing site, and several smaller UFOs arrive before a "mother ship" lands. Formerly abducted humans emerge—including Guiler's young son, who now reunites with his mom—and aliens descend and communicate with humans. A thrilled Neary climbs up the ramp and goes off to the stars with the aliens.

Christians can easily identify with Spielberg's portrayal of benign aliens whom the "powers that be" try to prevent us from being in contact with. The Bible tells us that the angels of God watch over us and lead us to salvation (see Hebrews 1:13–14) but, as Jesus said, "Many are called, but few are chosen" (Matthew 22:14 KJV). Man's societies often have an anti-God bias and seek to turn people away from the spiritual (see Matthew 23:13). Many who are called to God's kingdom get stopped and sidetracked and never have an "encounter" with God.

Don't let the world sidetrack you! Press on into the kingdom of God!

*Be all the more eager to make your calling
and election sure. For if you do these things,
you will never fall, and you will receive a rich
welcome into the eternal kingdom of our Lord
and Savior Jesus Christ.*
2 PETER 1:10–11 NIV

TAKE TWO

Do you ever feel as if you are being waylaid from your calling? If so, try spending more time in the presence of Christ. He'll help you stay on the right path.

What can you do to help those who are looking for more than what the material world offers? How can you help these truth-seekers have the most wonderful encounter ever—with Christ?

I've seen this movie ❑

My Star Review ☆ ☆ ☆ ☆ ☆

DEAD
POETS
SOCIETY

Rated: PG

Released June 2, 1989

Written by Tom Schulman

Directed by Peter Weir

Distributed by Touchstone Pictures

Starring:

Robin Williams (John Keating)

Robert Sean Leonard (Neil Perry)

Ethan Hawke (Todd Anderson)

Josh Charles (Knox Overstreet)

Gale Hansen (Charlie Dalton)

Dylan Kussman (Richard Cameron)

CHOOSING CAPTAINS

Dead Poets Society, set in an upper-crust boys' school in 1959, features the unorthodox teaching methods of English instructor John Keating and the secret revival of an old literary club, the Dead Poets Society.

While the school's values include tradition, honor, discipline, and excellence, Keating models creativity, spontaneity, and individual daring. He challenges his students to look for the poetry within their own hearts and to "seize the day" (carpe diem)—to discover their true selves languishing beneath the stifling boundaries of expectations set by society, the school, their parents, and their peers. As a result, each student faces a different antagonist, undergoes a tailor-made transformation, and experiences a unique reward. For example, Todd must overcome his self-consciousness to find his creative voice; Neil must stand up to his father to pursue his dream as an actor; and Charlie faces the wrath of Headmaster Nolan when he publishes a defiant article in the school paper.

When tragedy occurs, the students are interrogated individually and played against each other to bring about Keating's termination. In a powerful closing scene, Keating returns to his classroom to pick up his belongings. One by one, the students stand on their desks and salute their mentor, quoting Walt Whitman's poem: "O Captain! My Captain!" Their beloved teacher leaves knowing that even though the boys have suffered, the authorities have not stolen the lessons he planted in their hearts.

Dead Poets Society is such an inspiring portrayal of audacity versus control that the audience might be tempted to adopt the philosophy of the movie. But the worldview promoted by Keating is not exactly synonymous with that of Jesus. The primacy of personal freedom and self-actualization are often idols that compete for our allegiance to the lordship of Jesus. Further, the Bible calls us to honor our parents (see Matthew 15:3–4), obey those who govern us (see Romans 13:1–3), and heed spiritual leadership (see 1 Thessalonians 5:12–13). Ultimate truth and personal destiny are not found simply by casting off restraint to do what is right in our own eyes but through submission to Christ.

Yet the Bible also presents another side: to resist conformity to the world (see Romans 12:1–2) and put the gospel ahead of every other human institution, whether religious (see Acts 5:28–30), political (see

Revelation 13), or familial (see Mark 10:29–30). Like Daniel, faithful followers of Christ do not bow to the idols or kings but stand on their desks and say, "O Lord, my Lord!"

> *Daniel. . .pays no attention to you, O king,*
> *or to the decree you put in writing.*
> *He still prays three times a day.*
> DANIEL 6:13 NIV

 **TAKE TWO**

Christ challenged the authorities of His day. In what ways did the boys' actions in this film mirror or differ from Christ's? Where's the boundary between nonconforming behavior and outright rebellion?

Many people live under an oppressive authority—be it a government, culture, or family member. How can you help these people find their voice in a way that can redeem both them and their oppressors?

I've seen this movie ❏

My Star Review ☆ ☆ ☆ ☆ ☆

elf

Rated: PG

Released November 7, 2003

Written by David Berenbaum

Directed by Jon Favreau

Distributed by New Line Cinema

Starring:

Will Ferrell (Buddy)

James Caan (Walter)

Bob Newhart (Papa Elf)

Edward Asner (Santa)

Mary Steenburgen (Emily)

Zooey Deschanel (Jovie)

Michael Lerner (Fulton)

Andy Richter (Morris)

FINDING YOURSELF HAS NEVER BEEN SO MUCH FUN

Elf is a laugh-aloud Christmas comedy featuring Will Ferrell, who combines childlike innocence and excessive wonder in one hilarious reaction after another.

Buddy (Ferrell) is a human raised by North Pole elves after Santa accidentally brings him home in his toy bag one Christmas Eve. Buddy believes he's one of Santa's helpers, but due to his stature, clumsiness, and general ineptitude as an elf, the truth about his origins finally comes out. So Buddy sets out in search of his true identity in New York City. The reunion with his dad—Walter, a stressed-out children's book publisher—ends poorly with the oversized elf being tossed out of the building.

At Gimbel's department store, Buddy, because of his appearance and enthusiasm, is mistaken for an employee in the North Pole section. There he makes a new friend in Jovie. When the store Santa shows up and Buddy exposes him as a fake, the ensuing brawl lands Buddy in jail. Walter bails him out, discovers that

Buddy is truly his son, and takes him home. After a series of ups and downs in their relationship, the movie climaxes in Central Park, where the main characters muster the Christmas spirit required to help the real Santa through a crisis involving his sleigh.

Elf nails questions of identity and belonging. Buddy deals with these questions the hard way, but is sustained in his quest by being centered in uninhibited joy and expectancy.

Elf enables us to have a good belly laugh while pondering some of the core questions common to humanity. Deep in our hearts, we want to "find ourselves," often without knowing what that means. The longing for home, purpose, and belonging can only be satisfied by God the Father.

When the lost son (Luke 15:11–32) trudged out of the pigpen and made his humbling trek home, it was not merely to find the shelter and sustenance of a servant-helper. Something in his soul was crying out for what he could never dare hope to receive—his father's exuberant embrace. Only then did he come to know true sonship. The contrast between his homecoming and that of Buddy's is noteworthy, but the desire and belief that one's personal identity comes clear by knowing our true Father is a point we all have in common. The Bible calls this the spirit of adoption as sons and daughters of *Abba*—the beloved Father in whose arms we are forever welcome.

*For you did not receive a spirit that makes you a slave
again to fear, but you received the Spirit of sonship.
And by him we cry, "Abba, Father."*
ROMANS 8:15 NIV

 **TAKE TWO**

If you're completely honest with yourself, what's the
primary foundation of your identity? Ask God how
you can find your complete identity in Him.

Do you know anyone like Buddy, someone who still
hasn't found what he or she is looking for? What
can you do to help that person find his or her way
"home"?

I've seen this movie ❑

My Star Review ☆ ☆ ☆ ☆ ☆

E.T.
THE EXTRA-TERRESTRIAL

Rated: PG
Released June 11, 1982
Written by Melissa Mathison
Directed by Steven Spielberg
Distributed by Universal Studios

Starring:

Henry Thomas (Elliot)
Robert MacNaughton (Michael)
Drew Barrymore (Gertie)
K. C. Martel (Greg)
Sean Frye (Steve)
C. Thomas Howell (Tyler)
Dee Wallace (Mary)
Peter Coyote (Keys)

ALIENS AND STRANGERS ON EARTH

Ten-year-old Elliot lives with his mother Mary, his brother Michael, and sister Gertie, but Michael and his friends treat Elliot as a pesky younger brother and exclude him from their games. Meanwhile, on a nearby forested hill, US government agents have surrounded a UFO, the occupants of which are out collecting botanical samples. The spaceship is forced to depart suddenly, leaving one of the foragers behind and this small alien, later dubbed "E.T.," makes his way down the hill toward Elliot's house.

A loner and outsider himself, Elliot finds, then hides the alien and begins forming a mystical connection with him, but soon his sister and brother get in on the secret. They learn that E.T. has unusual powers and want to keep him, but E.T. informs them that he longs to leave. Indeed, he *must* leave, as his strength is already beginning to fade, so he puts together a makeshift communication device, saying, "E.T. phone home." The kids smuggle him out of the house during Halloween and he goes to the hilltop and makes his call, but by now his power is nearly gone. Elliot tries to persuade him to stay, saying, "You could be happy here. I could take care of you," but E.T. only replies, "Home."

E.T. is captured by government agents and dies—but then, amazingly, revives. In the climax he flees with the kids, levitating their bicycles to get past a roadblock. Elliot tells Keys, a government agent, "He *needs* to go home," and together they watch the spaceship lift off and carry E.T. back to his own world. In the Bible, when Elijah told a group of prophets that it was time for him to "go home," they didn't want him to leave and insisted on following him. However, only his closest friend, Elisha, saw the chariot of fire swoop down and Elijah being carried up to heaven (see 2 Kings 2:1–15).

Like E.T. and Elijah, we are "aliens and strangers on earth" (Hebrews 11:13 NIV), and though we form deep bonds with friends and family down here, ultimately, we're seeking a better world. Sometimes the feelings of homesickness for heaven are nearly overpowering and the words of this old hymn resonate with us: "Swing low, sweet chariot, comin' for to carry me home." Heaven is our true home.

*They admitted that they were aliens and strangers
on earth. People who say such things show that they
are looking for a country of their own. . . . They were
longing for a better country—a heavenly one.*
HEBREWS 11:13–14, 16 NIV

🎬 TAKE TWO

Are there times when you feel like an outsider? In
such situations, do you bend your faith in order to
"fit in" or do you seek the presence of God and find
home in His peace?

Do you still grieve over others who have passed on to
heaven? How do those feelings differ when you look
at their leaving not as a departure, but a heavenly
homecoming?

I've seen this movie ❑

My Star Review ✩ ✩ ✩ ✩ ✩

ENCHANTED

| Rated: PG |
| Released November 21, 2007 |
| Written by Bill Kelly |
| Directed by Kevin Lima |
| Distributed by Walt Disney Studios |

Starring:

Amy Adams (Giselle)

Patrick Dempsey (Robert Philip)

James Marsden (Prince Edward)

Timothy Spall (Nathaniel)

Rachel Covey (Morgan Philip)

Susan Sarandon (Queen Narissa)

HOPE-FILLED ROMANTIC

Enchanted is a comedic mishmash of Disney references that won viewers over by clashing the romantic formulas of an animated fairy princess with the cynicism of a Manhattan divorce lawyer.

The story begins in Andalasia, an animated world of magical clichés where Princess Giselle is to be wed to Edward, whose ascent threatens the crown of the evil queen, Narissa. Narissa expels Giselle from Andalasia through a magic portal landing her smack in the middle of New York's chaotic streets, a place where "happily ever after" is nothing but a quaint cliché.

While waiting for her Prince to rescue her, Giselle meets Robert, whose immersion in the petty world of divorce court has left him jaded and certain that Giselle is mentally ill. Through a series of mishaps, crises, and rescues, Giselle finds true love in the real world. Meanwhile, she tutors Robert in the value of romance, to the point where this cynic is finally able to open his heart.

This fish-out-of-water tale invites us to roll our eyes

at the "la-la-land" worldview of naïve escapism while simultaneously infecting us with some of the hope and joy to which life's disappointments tend to harden us. Can genuine love break through like a stubborn weed through cracked concrete?

This seemingly harmless lark of a story contains a powerful challenge to the nature of Christian love and faith. On the one hand, it nails the shallow faith of dreamy-eyed sentimentalism that evaporates in the faintest breeze of testing. It also demonstrates the poverty of prenuptial-agreement relationships and the hollow unbelief of fashionable cynicism. Such options! Are we really caught between fairy-tale faith and "realistic" despair?

Yet truth shines through: Love and faith can and must survive the icy cold of this dead world and the fiery breath of the mythical dragon. Believers signify that clear-minded, pure-hearted Way with the cross of Christ. This love believes in the goodness of God when life is falling apart, and it loves sacrificially. The grace-gifted love and faithfulness that saw Jesus overcome death and the grave was prefigured long ago in Song of Songs 8:6–7 (NIV):

[Love] burns like blazing fire, like a mighty flame.
Many waters cannot quench love;
rivers cannot wash it away.

*If one were to give all the wealth of his house
for love, it would be utterly scorned.*

This is the story of our Prince, written by the Father, animated by the Spirit, made flesh by the Son. It's no fairy-tale story; this is as true as it gets.

*Dear friends, let us love one another,
for love comes from God.*
1 JOHN 4:7 NIV

 **TAKE TWO**

How does love portrayed in most fairy-tale stories or romance films differ from true Christian love? How is it the same?

When was the last time you experienced unconditional love? Who in your world right now is in need of such love? How can you share it with him or her?

I've seen this movie ❏

My Star Review ☆ ☆ ☆ ☆ ☆

END of the SPEAR

Rated: PG-13

Released January 20, 2006

Written by Bill Ewing, Bart Gavigan, and Jim Hanon

Directed by Jim Hanon

Distributed by Jungle Films LLC

Starring:

Louie Leonardo (Mincayani)

Christina Souza (Dayuma)

Chad Allen (Nate Saint/Steve Saint/Narrator)

Sean McGowan (Jim Elliot)

Cara Stoner (Marj Saint)

Beth Bailey (Elisabeth Elliot)

Stephen Caudill (Ed McCully)

Matt Lutz (Pete Fleming)

Patrick Zeller (Roger Youderian)

A WRONG MADE RIGHTEOUS

This movie, famous for its breathtaking scenery, tells the true story of the Waodani tribe, living in the remote rain forests of eastern Ecuador. The Waodani were infamous as the most violent society ever encountered by anthropologists. At the slightest provocation, they would not only kill outsiders and neighboring tribesmen, but their own members. They were dedicated to revenge killings. In 1956, Nate Saint and his missionary team decide to preach the gospel to them.

Initial contact seems to go well, but when Nate and his team land on a nearby beach, they are brutally speared to death. Marj Saint and the other widows grieve, but the death of Nate is especially hard on their young son, Steve, who loved his father dearly. Just the same, compelled by Christ's love, the women forgive their husbands' murderers. Then, led by a Waodani woman, Dayuma, who has become a Christian (and had been living with Nate's sister in Quito, Ecuador), they go live among the Waodani.

Referring to God by the Waodani name for the Creator (*Oenagongi*), Dayuma preaches the gospel in simple terms that her people understand, saying, "*Oenagongi* had a Son: Even though He was speared, He did not spear back."

Their words and their example of Christian forgiveness touch the Waodani. Within a few years, many tribal members are converted and give up their violent ways. But Mincayani has a terrible secret. When Steve is a grown man and returns to the tribe years later, the two are discussing Nate Saint's death when Mincayani confesses that *he* was the one who killed Steve's father. He hands him his spear and tells Steve to kill him in revenge. Mincayani says, "Do it! I killed your father! Do it!" Steve answers, "No one took my father's life. He gave it."

Steve had peace in his heart. He had already forgiven his father's nameless murderer, and now, when confronted with the man himself and learning the details of his father's final moments, he did not give in to a new sense of outrage and a burning desire for revenge.

Have you forgiven those who have maligned or harmed you? If you have, then you'll have peace that will keep you from being overcome with negative emotions.

The peace of God, which transcends all
understanding, will guard your hearts
and your minds in Christ Jesus.
PHILIPPIANS 4:7 NIV

🎬 TAKE TWO

Having been raised on revenge, Mincayani had extreme courage in confessing his murder of Nate Saint to Steve. Is God prompting you to confess a wrong you've done to someone else? If God so leads you to confront this individual, ask Him to give you the courage you need.

In order to be forgiven by God, we, too, need to forgive. Is there someone whom God has put on your heart to forgive? Don't wait. Do so today!

I've seen this movie ❏

My Star Review ☆ ☆ ☆ ☆ ☆

FRANKENSTEIN

Rated: Unrated

Released November 21, 1931

Written by John L. Balderston, Francis Edward Faragoh, Garrett Fort, Robert Florey (uncredited), and John Russell (uncredited)

Based on the novel *Frankenstein* by Mary Shelley and the play by Peggy Webling

Directed by James Whale

Distributed by Universal Pictures

Starring:

Colin Clive (Dr. Henry Frankenstein)

Mae Clarke (Elizabeth)

John Boles (Victor Mortiz)

Boris Karloff (Frankenstein's Monster)

Edward Van Sloan (Dr. Waldman)

Frederick Kerr (Baron Frankenstein)

Dwight Frye (Fritz)

Marilyn Harris (Little Maria)

MONSTER OBSESSIONS

In this 1931 classic, Dr. Frankenstein is so obsessed with creating a living being that he and his accomplice, Fritz, rob graves, steal the corpses, and cobble together body parts into one huge, ugly monstrosity. Dr. Frankenstein wants to implant the brain of a "good" person into his ghoulish creation, but the brain of a criminal gets used instead.

Elizabeth, Frankenstein's fiancée, is distraught that Frankenstein has been spending so much time locked away in his watchtower laboratory with his experiments instead of preparing for their wedding, so together with Victor Moritz and Dr. Waldman, goes to the tower to try to talk him out of his obsession. They arrive during a thunderstorm just as Frankenstein and Fritz raise the corpse high up on the operating table and lightning strikes, bringing it to life.

The monstrosity is not inherently evil but when frightened by Fritz, it becomes dangerous, so they lock it up in the dungeon. When Fritz provokes it again, Frankenstein's Monster strangles him; then when Dr.

Frankenstein is away preparing for his wedding, the Monster kills Dr. Waldman and drowns a young girl named Maria. Finally it turns on Frankenstein himself and tries to kill him by throwing him from a windmill. Dr. Frankenstein recovers, but a mob of terrified townspeople burn down the windmill, killing the Monster.

Today, "Frankenstein's Monster"—or simply *Frankenstein*—describes a creation that evades the control of and ultimately destroys its creator. King David was also nearly destroyed by a monster of his own making: He committed adultery with Bathsheba, had her husband killed, and failed to punish Ammon for raping Absalom's sister. All this affected Absalom, and he in turn murdered Ammon, committed adultery with ten of David's concubines, and started a civil war that killed thousands. (See 2 Samuel 12:9–12; 13:1–29; 15:1–14; 18:6–8.)

While we may not rob graves for body parts like Dr. Frankenstein or sin as seriously as David, we should be aware that *all* sin has consequences and can ultimately destroy us. Some bad health habits or addictions literally shorten our lives. Some poor choices, if we don't nip them in the bud, take on a life of their own and lead to disaster. Let's repent of bad thoughts, habits, and sins before they become out of control.

*"Even now," declares the L*ORD*, "return to me with*
*all your heart. . . ." Return to the L*ORD *your God,*
for he is gracious and compassionate,
slow to anger and abounding in love,
and he relents from sending calamity.
JOEL 2:12–13 NIV

 **TAKE TWO**

Romans 12:2 instructs us to turn from the pattern
of this world and transform our minds. In what ways
can you endeavor to do this? Check out Romans
12:2 and discover why we are urged to take steps
toward a good thought life.

Have you made some bad choices or developed bad
habits that lead to negative consequences? What
did you learn from those situations? Where was
your focus during those times—on your wants or on
Jesus?

I've seen this movie ❑

My Star Review ☆ ☆ ☆ ☆ ☆

THE FUGITIVE

Rated: PG-13

Released August 6, 1993

Written by David Twohy and Jeb Stuart

Story by David Twohy

Directed by Andrew Davis

Distributed by Warner Bros.

Starring:

Harrison Ford (Dr. Richard Kimble)

Tommy Lee Jones (Chief Deputy Marshal Samuel Gerard)

Sela Ward (Helen Kimble)

Julianne Moore (Dr. Anne Eastman)

Joe Pantoliano (Deputy Marshal Cosmo Renfro)

Andreas Katsulas (Frederick Sykes)

Jeroen Krabbé (Dr. Charles Nichols)

Daniel Roebuck (Deputy Marshal Robert Biggs)

FINDING REFUGE

Dr. Richard Kimble, a happily married man and successful surgeon in the Chicago Memorial Hospital, comes home one night after performing an operation to find his wife, Helen, dying and a one-armed attacker fleeing. When Kimble is arrested for the murder, he discovers that he's been framed. His fingerprints are on the gun and bullets and there is no sign of a forced entry.

Having been sentenced to death by lethal injection, Kimble is being transferred on a bus to prison when another prisoner attacks a guard. In the confusion that follows, the bus driver is shot, the bus crashes, and Kimble escapes. Chief Deputy US Marshal Samuel Gerard and his team of US marshals are then assigned to rearrest him. Throughout this dramatic movie, Kimble barely stays one step ahead of his pursuers.

At one point, he is stopped by a police roadblock and escapes into a dam's drainage system. As he stands, trapped, at the edge of the spillway, Kimble tells Gerard, "I didn't kill my wife!" Gerard, whose job is to recapture Kimble, not solve the case, delivers the movie's most stinging line when he replies, "I don't care!" Kimble then leaps off the spillway into the water below, escaping.

Realizing he will always be thought guilty, Kimble determines to find out who actually killed his wife. He contacts his close friend, Dr. Charles Nichols—who, it turns out, was the one who betrayed him. Nichols stood to become rich by endorsing a new drug, Provasic, but Kimble's research showed that the drug was dangerous, so Nichols sent a one-armed hit man (Sykes) to kill Kimble's wife and pin the blame on Kimble. After a series of dramatic chases and fights, however, Sykes is defeated, Nichols arrested, and Kimble vindicated.

We sometimes feel like the fugitive: During our times of greatest need, it seems as though our friends just aren't there for us. "I looked on my right hand, and beheld, but there was no man that would know me: refuge failed me; no man cared for my soul" (Psalm 142:4 KJV). At times it feels like even God, by His silence, is saying, "I don't care," but this is never the case. God does care. As the rest of Psalm 142 states, God will never fail us.

When my spirit was overwhelmed within me,
*You knew my path. . . . I cried out to You, O L*ord*;*
I said, "You are my refuge, my portion
in the land of the living."
Psalm 142:3, 5 nasb

 **TAKE TWO**

Have you ever been unjustly accused? Did you feel
as if you were standing alone? Has what you learned
from that situation made you more empathetic to
others who feel misjudged or alone?

Do you have a friend who can see you through thick
and thin? If so, do you return the favor, lifting that
person up when he or she is low? If not, remember
you always have a friend in Jesus, so you are never
really alone.

I've seen this movie ❏

My Star Review ☆ ☆ ☆ ☆ ☆

GLADIATOR

Rated: R

Released May 5, 2000

Written by David Franzoni, John Logan, and
William Nicholson

Directed by Ridley Scott

Distributed by DreamWorks

Starring:

Russell Crowe (Maximus)

Joaquin Phoenix (Emperor Commodus)

Connie Nielsen (Lucilla)

Oliver Reed (Proximo)

Richard Harris (Emperor Marcus Aurelius)

Derek Jacobi (Gracchus)

Djimon Hounsou (Juba)

David Schofield (Falco)

FROM DARKNESS INTO LIGHT

This movie is based (loosely) upon historical facts, but gives a clear look into the pagan Roman mindset and desire for eternal life. In the movie, General Maximus leads the Roman army to victory over German barbarians in 180 AD and the wise, elderly Emperor Marcus Aurelius then appoints Maximus ruler in place of his son Commodus. Commodus, however, murders his father and orders Maximus killed.

Maximus escapes but returns to Rome to find his wife and son murdered, after which he is captured by slavers, bought by Proximo, and trained to fight as a gladiator. Eventually, he is brought back to Rome to fight in the Coliseum, where he leads Proximo's team of gladiators to victory. When Commodus asks who the mysterious gladiator is, Maximus boldly reveals himself. Commodus fears Maximus, but can't put him to death because he's too popular with the crowd. Later, when Commodus pits Maximus against the city's greatest gladiator, Maximus wins by a narrow margin.

In the end, Commodus himself battles Maximus in the arena—after first puncturing the latter's lung with a stiletto—but Maximus still defeats him; then, as Maximus dies, his spirit departs for *Elysium* (the Roman equivalent of heaven) to be reunited with his wife and family.

Maximus epitomizes the ideal pagan who honored the gods, valued strength and honor, and gladly fought for the glory of the Empire. Maximus declares that while "the rest of the world. . .is brutal and cruel and dark, Rome is the light." By 180 AD, however, untold thousands of Romans had become disillusioned with the pagan ideals Maximus espoused and had turned to the *true* Light, Jesus.

Commodus deserved his bad reputation: Secular history describes him as an extreme egotist with neurotic problems. However, historians fondly remember Marcus Aurelius as the last of the "Five Good Emperors." How differently Christians remember him! *Halley's Bible Handbook* tells us that Marcus Aurelius—to uphold worship of Roman gods—encouraged "cruel and barbarous" persecutions of Christians in which thousands perished.

Yet in the end, the Christians triumphed. Rome, with its pagan gods and ideals, was not the light, but Jesus Christ "was the *true* Light" (John 1:9 NASB, emphasis added). Jesus died to fulfill the longings of pagans, like Maximus, who yearned for a happy afterlife in which they could be reunited with loved ones. Two thousand years later, Jesus still offers light and life to the weary world.

> *I am the light of the world:*
> *he that followeth me shall not walk in darkness,*
> *but shall have the light of life.*
> JOHN 8:12 KJV

 **TAKE TWO**

Does the thought of heaven comfort you? How do you envision this wonderful place?

Do you know of someone who is living in darkness? What can you do to help them see the Light of Jesus?

I've seen this movie ❏

My Star Review ☆ ☆ ☆ ☆ ☆

GONE WITH THE WIND

Rated: G

Released December 15, 1939

Written by Sidney Howard; (uncredited) contributing writers Oliver H. P. Garrett, Ben Hecht, Jo Swerling, and John Van Druten

Based on the novel by Margaret Mitchell

Directed by Victor Fleming, George Cukor (uncredited), and Sam Wood (uncredited)

Distributed by Metro-Goldwyn-Mayer

Starring:

Thomas Mitchell (Gerald O'Hara)

Vivien Leigh (Scarlett O'Hara)

Clark Gable (Rhett Butler)

Olivia de Havilland (Melanie Hamilton Wilkes)

Rand Brooks (Charles Hamilton)

Carroll Nye (Frank Kennedy)

Hattie McDaniel (Mammy)

Leslie Howard (Ashley Wilkes)

LOOKING FOR LOVE
IN ALL THE WRONG PLACES

Scarlett O'Hara, a strong-willed, flirtatious young woman, is living on her family's plantation in Twelve Oaks, Georgia, at the outbreak of the Civil War. Scarlett asks Ashley Wilkes to marry her—but he tells her that though he has feelings for her, he and her cousin Melanie are more compatible. Rhett Butler overhears the conversation and thus begins his long love-hate relationship with Scarlett.

Melanie marries Ashley, and Scarlett marries Melanie's brother, Charles, just before he heads off to war. After Charles dies, Rhett shows up on furlough and declares his love for Scarlett—but she insists they'll never marry. Instead, she shares a passionate, stolen kiss with Ashley. When the war ends, Scarlett works hard in her family's cotton fields to survive. She declares, "If I have to lie, steal, cheat, or kill, as God is my witness, I'll never be hungry again!"

When Ashley returns from the war, Scarlett urges him to run off with her, but he refuses to abandon

Melanie. Then, hearing that Rhett is now wealthy, Scarlett proposes marriage to him, but when she learns that his assets are frozen, she lies to her sister's fiancé—the successful businessman Frank Kennedy—steals him from her sister and marries him. After Frank is killed, Rhett again proposes and he and Scarlett are finally married. After a period of initial happiness however, Rhett realizes that his wife is still in love with Ashley.

In the end, Melanie dies. Then, seeing the intensity of Ashley's grief, Scarlett realizes she'd never had a chance with Ashley and she does truly love Rhett. But Rhett, thoroughly disgusted, walks out, leaving Scarlett utterly alone.

God compared the nation of Israel to His wife: He had given her everything she needed, yet the foolish Israelites determined to follow the lascivious god Baal. God eventually restored His relationship with Israel, but only after she'd suffered greatly (see Hosea 2:1–17). Christians can be guilty of straying as well. As Jesus warned, "I hold this against you: You have forsaken your first love" (Revelation 2:4 NIV).

We wish for all stories to have happy endings, but for that to happen we must realize that what we have is so much better than any illicit longings we entertain.

*She will chase after her lovers but not catch them;
she will look for them but not find them. Then she
will say, "I will go back to my husband as at first, for
then I was better off than now."*
HOSEA 2:7 NIV

■ TAKE TWO

Do you think the adage "the grass is greener on the
other side of the fence" is a true statement? If so,
how can we change that mind-set?

Have you ever coveted something you couldn't—nor
shouldn't—have, and then obtained it? Or was the
coveted item forever out of your reach? In either
situation, how did you feel? How can you keep your
passion for Jesus and the Word from growing cold?

I've seen this movie ❏

My Star Review ☆ ☆ ☆ ☆ ☆

HIGH NOON

Rated: Unrated

Released July 30, 1952

Written by Carl Foreman

Based on the story by John W. Cunningham

Directed by Fred Zinnemann

Distributed by United Artists

Starring:

Gary Cooper (Marshall Will Kane)

Grace Kelly (Amy Fowler Kane)

Lloyd Bridges (Deputy Marshal Harvey Pell)

Katy Jurado (Helen Ramírez)

Ian MacDonald (Frank Miller)

Thomas Mitchell (Mayor Jonas Henderson)

Morgan Farley (Dr. Mahin, the minister)

Otto Kruger (Judge Percy Mettrick)

THE COURAGE OF CONVICTION

Years earlier, Marshall Will Kane of Hadleyville in New Mexico territory arrested a killer, Frank Miller, and Judge Mettrick sentenced him to prison. However, Miller has been released and is on his way back to town to kill Kane and Mettrick. His old gang arrives to meet him. Meanwhile, Will Kane has just retired and married Amy Fowler, who converted to the pacifistic Quaker faith when her father and brother were gunned down. Together, Will and Amy plan on settling down in peace.

When they learn Miller is arriving at noon to kill Kane and Mettrick, the judge packs up and leaves, saying, "This is just a dirty little village in the middle of nowhere. Nothing that happens here is really important. Now get out." In other words, it's not worth risking your life for. The townspeople themselves urge Kane to flee since he's no longer marshall, but Kane says, "I've got to stay. Anyway, I'm the same man with or without this." He then pins his badge back on his vest.

Kane's deputy, Harvey Pell, resigns, and Kane goes

to the saloon to enlist deputies, but is mocked. He interrupts a church service to find support, but no one joins him. His friends either hide from him or give excuses; even his new bride, Amy, buys a ticket to leave town. Kane faces the four outlaws alone and the firefight begins, but Amy, hearing the shots, returns and shoots a gunman. When all four outlaws are dead and Kane's mission ends, he throws his badge in the dust and leaves with his wife.

Paul knew what it was like to stand alone. He had evangelized hundreds in the Roman province of Asia and watched over them for years, but in the end, all of them deserted him. When he stood trial before Nero, even his close friends abandoned him (2 Timothy 1:15). Paul said, "No one stood with me, but all forsook me." Then he added, "But the *Lord* stood with me and strengthened me" (2 Timothy 4:16–17 NKJV, emphasis added).

There will be times when we need to stand up for some issue, and our friends might choose not to stand with us. That's when we need the courage and faith to stand alone simply because it's the right thing to do.

*Indeed the hour is coming, yes, has now come,
that you will be scattered, each to his own,
and will leave Me alone. And yet I am not alone,
because the Father is with Me.*
JOHN 16:32 NKJV

 **TAKE TWO**

Have you ever found yourself standing alone? During those times we need to listen, as did Elijah in 1 Kings 19, for God to give us direction and comfort.

What do you do when you need courage? Replenish yourself with prayer and reading of the Word. The Bible tells us to "fear not" 365 times—one verse for each day of the year!

I've seen this movie ❏

My Star Review ☆ ☆ ☆ ☆ ☆

HOME ALONe

Rated: PG
Released November 16, 1990
Written by John Hughes
Directed by Chris Columbus
Distributed by 20th Century Fox

Starring:

Macaulay Culkin (Kevin McCallister)
John Heard (Peter McCallister)
Catherine O'Hara (Kate McCallister)
Joe Pesci (Harry)
Daniel Stern (Marv)
Hillary Wolf (Megan McCallister)
Angela Goethals (Linnie McCallister)
Devin Ratray (Buzz McCallister)

STANDING IN THE BREACH

It's the day before the McCallister family flies out to Paris for a Christmas vacation and eight-year-old Kevin feels like everyone is picking on him. When he quarrels with his older brother Buzz, his mother, Kate, sends him up to the attic bedroom for the night. He shouts down at her, "I don't want any family. . . . I don't want to see you again for the rest of my whole life!" When she replies that he'd feel pretty sad if he woke up the next morning and didn't have a family, Kevin retorts, "No, I wouldn't!"

That night, a power outage messes up the alarm clocks and the McCallisters wake up so late that they scramble to catch their flight. They make it, but half-way across the Atlantic Kate realizes they've forgotten Kevin! As soon as they arrive in Paris, the family is in a mad scramble to get back home as quickly as possible.

Meanwhile, Kevin finds everyone gone and says gleefully, "I made my family disappear!" During the next days, with no one to answer to, he stuffs himself with junk food and watches horror movies. But trouble comes when two thieves, Harry and Marv, try to invade the McCallisters' house. It's up to Kevin to defend his home—and defend it he does, defeating them with ice, red-hot doorknobs, a BB gun, gangster movies, and broken Christmas tree ornaments! By the time Kevin's family returns, they've all learned some deep lessons about the importance of family.

In the Bible, Gilead had an illegitimate son named Jephthah. When Gilead's other sons grew up, they drove Jephthah out of their family, saying that he'd never share the inheritance with them. Yet Jephthah was a mighty warrior, and when the land of Gilead was overrun by invaders, it was to Jephthah that the elders turned, seeking a leader to defend their homeland. (See Judges 11:1–11; 12:7.)

When a family member gets on our nerves or offends us, we're tempted to give him or her the cold shoulder or exclude the person from family gatherings, but it's best to forgive instead of feud. Not only does it make for more loving, peaceful relations, but you never know when you'll need that "despised" family member's help!

*But Jephthah said to the elders of Gilead,
"Did you not hate me, and drive me out of my
father's house? Why have you come to me
now when you are in trouble?"*
JUDGES 11:7 RSV

 TAKE TWO

What do you do when a family member gets on your nerves? Do you count to ten, giving yourself time to calm down, keeping yourself from saying words you can't take back? If you need more time, try silently reciting the books of the Bible.

Ruptured family relationships can make everyone in that family miserable. What can you do today to repair any breach?

I've seen this movie ❑

My Star Review ☆ ☆ ☆ ☆ ☆

HOOSIERS

Rated: PG

Released November 14, 1986

Written by Angelo Pizzo

Directed by David Anspaugh

Distributed by Orion Pictures

Starring:

Gene Hackman (Coach Norman Dale)

Barbara Hershey (Myra Fleener)

Dennis Hopper (Shooter)

Sheb Wooley (Cletus)

Fern Persons (Opal Fleener)

Chelcie Ross (George)

Robert Swan (Rollin)

Michael O'Guinne (Rooster)

John Robert Thompson (Sheriff Finley)

Michael Sassone (Preacher Purl)

"MORE THAN CONQUERORS"

Hoosiers is based upon the true story of a small-town Indiana basketball team that rose to challenge the top teams in its state and, against all odds, to win the championship. What makes the team members' achievement all the more remarkable is that they were led to victory by a sports coach, Norman Dale, who had seen better days, together with Shooter, the town drunkard. Whether or not you're a sports fan, this is such an inspirational movie that you must see it.

Dale upsets the status quo when he begins as new coach of Hickory High in 1951. He dismisses the interim coach and a basketball player within minutes of taking over, and begins training his undisciplined team. He has his players run for hours without shooting a ball. His controversial training methods seem to have little to do with basketball, and after he loses several games, his critics call a meeting to fire him. Dale's job is saved when team members say they'll only play basketball if he remains as coach.

Dale goes on to lead his team from victory to victory, but winning the state championship turns out to be only part of the goal. As Coach Dale tells his team, "If you put your effort and concentration into playing to your potential, to be the best that you can be, I don't care what the scoreboard says at the end of the game, in my book we're gonna be winners."

The Bible emphasizes this same principle, telling us that all we must do is remain faithful to God, to continue to believe in Jesus no matter how life's "scoreboard" says we're doing. If we do that, then Christ will do what we cannot do—give us spiritual victory over the world and all the forces of the enemy arrayed against us.

Often when we appear to be on a losing streak, we wonder if God has lifted His blessing from us because we're such a failure, or because He no longer loves us. But the Bible tells us hard times and even failures are part of our discipline and training, and are necessary to make us the Christians we need to be. (See Hebrews 12:3–12.)

Yes, God still loves you and has a plan for you, even when you seem to be losing.

If God is for us, who can be against us?. . .
Yet in all these things we are more than
conquerors through Him who loved us.
ROMANS 8:31, 37 NKJV

🎬 TAKE TWO

Have you ever felt like a failure, beaten down and
discouraged by experiences in your life? God is
always with us—before and after the battle. Spend
some time with Him today, asking Him to give you
the strength, encouragement, and hope you need to
walk His way.

Are you currently living to your full potential? If not,
what can you do to change that? Remember Christ
wants us to have an abundant life. He's doing His
part. Will you do yours?

I've seen this movie ❏

My Star Review ☆ ☆ ☆ ☆ ☆

THE INCREDIBLE HULK

Rated: PG-13

Released June 13, 2008

Written by Edward Norton and Zak Penn

Comic book by Stan Lee and Jack Kirby

Directed by Louis Leterrier

Distributed by Universal Studios

Starring:

Edward Norton (Bruce Banner)

Liv Tyler (Betty Ross)

William Hurt (General Thaddeus "Thunderbolt" Ross)

Tim Roth (Emil Blonsky)

Tim Blake Nelson ("Mr. Blue"/Samuel Sterns)

Ty Burrel (Leonard Samson)

Lou Ferrigno (The Incredible Hulk)

Débora Nascimento (Martina)

TAMING THE BEAST WITHIN

Bruce Banner was a scientist working on a military experiment, who, after subjecting himself to a dose of gamma radiation, transformed into a superhuman monster called the Hulk. Banner has an anger problem and, as he soon discovers, each time he gives in to rage, he transforms into a green-skinned monster. Unable to deal with the beast within, he runs off.

The movie opens some years later in Brazil, where Banner has chosen a simple life with the working-class poor and is studying martial arts to help control his anger. He is also in contact with a scientist, "Mr. Blue," whom he hopes will find a cure for his condition. General Ross has not given up hunting for him, however, and one day an accident in the factory leads Ross and his commandos to Banner.

After becoming angry and battering his pursuers, Hulk ends up back in America, where he gets in touch with his former girlfriend, Betty Ross. Meanwhile, one of the commandos, Emil Blonsky, persuades General Ross to give him a gamma treatment so he can fight the Hulk. That, together with a second treatment by Mr. Blue, turns Blonsky into a superhuman monstrosity.

Banner transforms into the Hulk to fight Blonsky and is about to strangle him with a chain when, see-ing Betty's shocked reaction, lets him go—proving that even in his enraged state, Hulk can exert willpower to control his anger. Hulk later transforms back into Bruce Banner, and stays human by controlling his anger.

This not only works for the Hulk, but for all of us. We can choose to not give in to anger. When Betty shouts an obscenity at a motorist, Banner chides, "I know a few techniques that could help you manage that anger very effectively." The Bible also has some ef-fective techniques to control anger, telling us to "cease from anger, and forsake wrath" (Psalm 37:8 KJV).

Self-control is one of the fruits of the Spirit (see Galatians 5:22–23), meaning that when the Spirit of Christ lives in our hearts, He gives us the ability to be patient. He gives us the power to forsake wrath. It takes time and patience to develop healthy habits, however. We must reinforce the habit by continually, consciously choosing to let go of anger.

Get rid of all bitterness, rage and anger, brawling and slander, along with every form of malice. Be kind and compassionate to one another, forgiving each other, just as in Christ God forgave you.
EPHESIANS 4:31–32 NIV

 **TAKE TWO**

Do you find yourself losing your cool when you're driving? How can you "temper" your reactions to those with whom you share the road—or with those you meet on the way?

Sometimes, when angry, we say things we can never take back. Have you found yourself regretting rash words spoken in haste? Ask God to help you rein in your tongue. And if you do slip up, be quick to ask forgiveness.

I've seen this movie ❑

My Star Review ☆ ☆ ☆ ☆ ☆

INDEPENDENCE DAY

Rated: PG-13

Released July 3, 1996

Written by Dean Devlin and Roland Emmerich

Directed by Roland Emmerich

Distributed by 20th Century Fox

Starring:

Will Smith (Captain Steven Hiller)

Bill Pullman (President Thomas J. Whitmore)

Jeff Goldblum (David Levinson)

Mary McDonnell (First Lady Marilyn Whitmore)

Judd Hirsch (Julius Levinson)

Robert Loggia (General William Grey)

Randy Quaid (Russell Casse)

Margaret Colin (Constance Spano)

Vivica A. Fox (Jasmine Dubrow)

BATTLING THE DESTROYER

aptain Steven Hiller is a US Marine Corps F/A-18 pilot. When alien destroyers begin attacking Earth, Hiller is just the kind of man you'd expect to rise to help lead the human resistance. His training and experience has prepared him for this moment. David Levinson is another likely hero: A computer expert working as a satellite technician, he uncovers the aliens' invasion timetable and comes up with a plan to defeat them. Thomas J. Whitmore is the US president and a former fighter pilot in the Persian Gulf War, so you aren't surprised when he personally flies a jet to attack the aliens' ships.

The *unlikely* hero in *Independence Day* is Russell Casse, a former Vietnam War pilot and a widower who's raising his three children alone. While this has the makings of a hero, Casse's "problems" work against him. His oldest child has little respect for him, for Casse is an alcoholic and, worse yet, for ten years he's made outlandish claims of having been abducted by aliens. Casse's claims suddenly seem very credible now.

While the other characters are fighting for survival, Casse has a personal motive to counterattack. As he flies toward an alien destroyer, he says the classic line: "Ha, ha, ha! Hello, boys! I'm back!" When his missile jams and won't fire, Casse rams his jet into an opening in the underbelly of the ship, sacrificing himself to wipe out the aliens. He has found their weak spot, and later pilots use this knowledge to wipe out the destroyers.

It's not difficult to find a parallel between these aliens—who travel from planet to planet, destroying all life—and demonic forces out to destroy humanity. One of Satan's chief demons is Apollyon, the Destroyer (see Revelation 9:11), and like Casse, many of us have been abducted by the devil, "having been taken captive by him to do his will" (2 Timothy 2:26 NKJV)—whether to destroy ourselves through drugs, promiscuous sex, the occult, or other snares of Satan.

Having found freedom in Jesus Christ, we are now fully aware of the stratagems the devil uses to ensnare people. We know what his end game is. We know that Satan is the destroyer. When it comes time to rise up and fight, we are motivated. This is personal.

We do not wrestle against flesh and blood, but against principalities, against powers, against the rulers of the darkness of this age, against spiritual hosts of wickedness in the heavenly places.
EPHESIANS 6:12 NKJV

◼ TAKE TWO

Have you ever found yourself in a battle against destructive forces? What did you do to combat them? Were you successful? Sometimes all we can do is remain faithful in God, knowing that He is the one who will save us and fight our battle (see 1 Samuel 17:47).

Have you ever stood up to evil when you were afraid? God gives us courage. But we need to be armed. Before stepping into the fray, don't forget to put on your armor (see Ephesians 6:10–18).

I've seen this movie ❏

My Star Review ☆ ☆ ☆ ☆ ☆

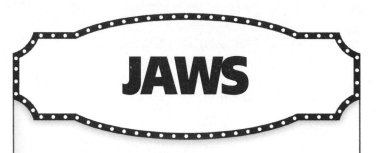

JAWS

Rated: PG

Released June 20, 1975

Written by Peter Benchly, Carl Gottlieb, and
   Howard Sackler (uncredited)

Based on the novel by Peter Benchley

Directed by Steven Spielberg

Distributed by Universal Pictures

Starring:

Roy Scheider (Police Chief Martin Brody)

Robert Shaw (Captain Quint)

Richard Dreyfuss (Matt Hooper)

Lorraine Gary (Ellen Brody)

Jeffrey Kramer (Deputy Leonard "Lenny"
Hendricks)

Murray Hamilton (Mayor Larry Vaughn)

Susan Backlinie (Christine "Chrissie" Watkins)

Jeffrey Voorhees (Alex Kintner)

Chris Rebello (Michael Brody)

"LOOKING FOR SOMEONE TO DEVOUR"

One night at the beach town of Amity Island in New England, young Chrissie Watkins decides to go for a dip in the ocean. Suddenly she cries out in pain and fear and is pulled under. The next morning her mangled remains wash up, and later the coroner announces she was killed by a shark. Police Chief Martin Brody begins putting up signs warning people not to go in the water, but all Mayor Vaughn and the local merchants can think about is lost revenue from beach-goers, so he persuades the coroner to alter his report, and the signs are taken down.

The next day the beaches are crowded when the shark strikes again, dragging under a young boy. His distraught mother posts a reward for whoever kills the monster and soon a host of bounty hunters descend on the community. When a tiger shark is caught, everyone breathes a sigh of relief. Matt Hooper of the Oceanographic Institute, however, believes that the teeth marks match a great white, but he is unable to persuade the mayor.

On July 4th the shark strikes again, this time killing a local boater. Hooper and Brody persuade the mayor to hire a professional fisherman named Quint to hunt the shark, so Hooper and Brody head out with Quint. They find the shark and it attacks, devouring Quint and sinking his ship, but Brody lodges an air tank in the monster's jaws, then detonates it with a rifle shot. With the shark dead, Brody and Hooper paddle back to shore.

The Bible warns us of a deadly foe who lurks unseen in the spiritual realm. Like the great white shark in the movie, our adversary, the devil, is powerful, very cunning, and looking for someone to devour. One reason he is able to continue his dirty work, claiming one victim after another, is because most people choose to believe that he doesn't exist. Don't be ignorant of his ploys (see 2 Corinthians 2:11)!

Like Hooper and Brody, we must take Satan's spiritual attacks seriously, stand up to him in Jesus' name, and drive him off. We can't kill him, but the Bible tells us "Resist the devil, and he *will* flee from you" (James 4:7 KJV, emphasis added).

*Stay sober, stay alert! Your enemy, the Adversary,
stalks about like a roaring lion looking
for someone to devour.*
1 PETER 5:8 CJB

🎬 TAKE TWO

In the same way Mayor Vaughn ignored all the
warning signs of a killer shark, Cain ignored God's
warning (see Genesis 4:7), which led to Abel's
demise. Have you ever ignored the evidence and
let sin get the better of you? How can you prevent
doing so in the future?

How can you protect yourself from Satan's wiles?
Do as Christ did. When you are under attack,
quote Scripture. Do you have some good verses
memorized? If not, begin doing so today.

I've seen this movie ❑

My Star Review ☆ ☆ ☆ ☆ ☆

JUNO

Rated: PG-13
Released December 5, 2007
Written by Diablo Cody
Directed by Jason Reitman
Distributed by Fox Searchlight Pictures

Starring:

Ellen Page (Juno MacGuff)
Michael Cera (Paulie Bleeker)
Jennifer Garner (Vanessa Loring)
Jason Bateman (Mark Loring)
Alison Janney (Brenda MacGuff)
J. K. Simmons (Mac MacGuff)
Olivia Thirlby (Leah)

BEYOND OURSELVES

Juno is a "dramedy" that traces the adult choices of Juno MacGuff, a sixteen-year-old high-schooler from Minnesota, who discovers she is pregnant via her friend Paulie. Juno's first instinct is to get an abortion, but she changes her mind and locates a couple interested in adopting her baby. Juno's early contacts with Vanessa (the prospective mom) are awkward, but she connects well with Mark, the potential dad. Unfortunately, Mark's interest in Juno becomes romantic, and although she extracts herself from that relationship, the marriage ends up dissolving. Again, Juno is confronted with a decision about what to do with the child: Should she keep the baby? Or proceed with the adoption with a soon-to-be-single Vanessa?

Much of the buzz for this movie focused on Juno's choice to reject abortion in favor of adoption. The movie received both acclaim and criticism from both pro-life and pro-choice camps for promoting choice but rejecting abortion. *Juno* reflected the growing refusal of people to be co-opted by the idealism of either tribe, acknowledging the impasse in the culture wars while searching for some common ground that honors both a mother's choice and the child's life. How Juno navigates this mess is the meat of the film.

That said, one can forever tinker with social hot buttons yet fail to see the bigger picture of what drives us to one camp or another. *Juno* is a good parable of what lies behind godly values and how easily those same values might evaporate in real-life contexts.

While many Christians applaud Juno's choice to adopt and many others defend her right to choose, all of us ought to ask *how* she made her decision. We should ask this same question of ourselves. Are we merely acting on our own whims, following our hearts (see Numbers 15:39) and doing what is right in our own eyes (see Judges 17:6)? Or at some point, does the will of God (the commands of Christ) trump the demands of personal convenience?

Juno's wisdom is her ability to look beyond how every decision will affect her. The baby matters, Vanessa matters, Paulie matters—she is thinking beyond her own self-interest. Conversely, Mark represents the fruit of self-seeking and a life that is "all about me." Today, let us seek to orbit God's agenda rather than asking Him to spin around our own wants and needs.

*Trust in the L*ORD *with all your heart*
and lean not on your own understanding;
in all your ways acknowledge him,
and he will make your paths straight.
PROVERBS 3:5–6 NIV

TAKE TWO

How would you describe God's role in your decision-making process? Think back on some key decisions you've made recently. What informed those choices?

Consider a significant decision you're facing right now. Who are all of the other people who will be impacted by this decision? What steps can you take to ensure the outcome of your decision is a win-win situation?

I've seen this movie ❑

My Star Review ☆ ☆ ☆ ☆ ☆

JURASSIC PARK

Rated: PG-13

Released June 11, 1993

Written by Michael Crichton, David Koepp, and
Malia Scotch Marmo

Based on the novel by Michael Crichton

Directed by Steven Spielberg

Distributed by Universal Pictures

Starring:

Sam Neill (Dr. Alan Grant)

Laura Dern (Dr. Ellie Sattler)

Jeff Goldblum (Dr. Ian Malcolm)

Richard Attenborough (John Hammond)

Bob Peck (Robert Muldoon)

Martin Ferrero (Donald Gennaro)

Joseph Mazzello (Tim Murphy)

Ariana Richards (Alexis "Lex" Murphy)

Wayne Knight (Dennis Nedry)

YOU COULD—BUT SHOULD YOU?

John Hammond, CEO of InGen, has done the impossible—he's brought dinosaurs back to life. His method was ingenious: He found prehistoric mosquitoes preserved inside amber, then extracted dinosaur blood from them and used the fossilized DNA (with frog DNA spliced in to fill the missing sequences) to re-create dinosaurs. Hammond then created a theme park, planning to charge visitors to see these wonders.

When a worker is killed by velociraptors, however, Hammond brings in experts to reassure his jittery investors and endorse Jurassic Park. These experts are paleontologist Alan Grant, paleobotanist Ellie Sattler, chaos theorist Ian Malcolm, and attorney Donald Gennaro. After seeing some dinosaurs, Malcolm expresses profound reservations, but the attorney exclaims, "We're gonna make a fortune with this place!"

The park's chief computer programmer, Dennis Nedry, is also driven by greed, and has received a bribe from InGen's rival to deliver dinosaur embryos to them. Nedry creates havoc when, to steal frozen embryos, he shuts down the park's security system; with the electricity gone from the fences, dinosaurs begin escaping, and kill and injure humans. In the end, after a series of harrowing adventures, Grant and the other experts decide *not* to endorse Jurassic Park.

Many Christians today are concerned when genetic engineers tamper with God's created order (see Genesis 1:12, 21, 24) to invent new species, even splicing animal DNA into vegetables. While many of these creations have the potential for good, the chief driving force is usually enormous profits. This causes companies to push across ethical lines with little regard for the consequences. As Ian Malcolm said in the movie, "Your scientists were so preoccupied with whether or not they *could*, they didn't stop to think if they *should*."

This principle applies to us in all areas of ethics that we, as Christians, encounter in life. For example, the Bible tells us that "for the sake of conscience" (Romans 13:5 AMP) we are to pay our taxes. Certainly we can take advantage of legitimate tax exemptions, but Christians should pay their taxes honestly. This also applies to what we watch on TV or view on the Internet. We could watch a lot of things, but *should* we? In all that we do, let's be motivated by biblical ethical standards and God's love.

*For the love of money is a root of all kinds of evil,
for which some have strayed from the faith
in their greediness, and pierced themselves
through with many sorrows.*
1 TIMOTHY 6:10 NKJV

 **TAKE TWO**

Was there ever a time when you had to separate
your greed from your conscience? What were the
circumstances and how was the situation resolved?
Which mind-set won out and what consequence
resulted?

What action can you take to support companies that
maintain ethical standards—for the sake of your
conscience? How can you set an example for your
children in that regard?

I've seen this movie ❏

My Star Review ☆ ☆ ☆ ☆ ☆

KING KONG

Rated: PG-13

Released December 14, 2005

Written by Peter Jackson, Fran Walsh, and
   Philippa Boyens

Based on a story by Merian C. Cooper and Edgar
   Wallace

Directed by Peter Jackson

Distributed by Universal Pictures

Starring:

Naomi Watts (Ann Darrow)

Jack Black (Carl Denham)

Adrien Brody (Jack Driscoll)

Thomas Kretschmann (Captain Englehorn)

Jamie Bell (Jimmy)

Kyle Chandler (Bruce Baxter)

Andy Serkis (Kong/Lumpy)

Evan Parke (Ben Hayes)

Colin Hanks (Preston)

MANIPULATING MONSTERS

The Great Depression is on, Carl Denham is out to make a movie, and he doesn't care who he has to use to do it. He escapes from New York City on a steamer just before alarmed investors can stop him. He promises Captain Englehorn money he doesn't have. He cons actress Ann Darrow into making a movie in Singapore—when they're actually headed to Skull Island. He tricks scriptwriter Jack Driscoll into coming along by keeping him on board until the ship leaves.

When they reach Skull Island, Ann is captured by savages and offered as a sacrifice to King Kong, a twenty-five-foot-tall gorilla. Denham wants to capture everything on film, so he talks Englehorn into leading a rescue party to find Ann. As crew members begin dying—first Mike, then Herb—Denham gushes with false promises, saying, "We're gonna finish this film for Herb. And we'll donate the proceeds to his wife and kids."

When the group is forced to turn back, Jack Driscoll continues on alone to find Ann. Denham is happy to let Jack and Ann serve as bait and prepares chloroform to sedate King Kong when the ape returns in hot pursuit of the couple. Sure enough, Kong is captured and taken to New York, where Denham charges people money to see him.

After Kong breaks free, he is reunited with Ann, but when the military is sent out to kill him, he climbs to the top of the Empire State Building. There, airplanes riddle him with bullets, and Kong falls to the street below. Carl Denham walks up and says, "It wasn't the airplanes. It was *beauty* killed the beast," but Jack Driscoll has it right when he says, "That's the thing you come to learn about Carl, his undying ability to destroy the things he loves."

The Bible warns against ruthless teachers who "speak great swelling words" but whose end goal is to "make merchandise of you" (2 Peter 2:18, 3 KJV). Beware of such men! We should also examine our *own* motives and make sure that we're not using others. It's fine to ask others for help and favors, but we cross the line when we manipulate or deceive to get them to do what we want. Don't be guilty of that!

False prophets also arose among the people, just as there will also be false teachers among you. . .and in their greed they will exploit you with false words.
2 PETER 2:1, 3 NASB

🎬 TAKE TWO

Have you ever found yourself, perhaps unconsciously, manipulating someone to get what you want? What can you do to prevent that from happening in the future?

As a Christian, do you find it hard to say no when someone asks you for help or for a favor? How can you keep others from manipulating you? Perhaps the wisest course may be to postpone an answer until you've prayed about it. Then simply trust God to give you direction.

I've seen this movie ❑

My Star Review ☆ ☆ ☆ ☆ ☆

LIARLIAR

Rated: PG-13
Released March 21, 1997
Written by Paul Guay and Stephen Mazur
Directed by Tom Shadyac
Distributed by Universal Pictures

Starring:

Jim Carrey (Fletcher Reede)

Maura Tierney (Audrey Reede)

Justin Cooper (Max Reede)

Cary Elwes (Jerry)

Jennifer Tilly (Samantha Cole)

Amanda Donohoe (Miranda)

Swoosie Kurtz (Dana Appleton)

Jason Bernard (Judge Marshall Stevens)

"THE TRUTH SHALL SET YOU FREE"

Fletcher Reede is a lawyer, divorced and overly dedicated to his job. He promises to be there for his young son Max's birthday party, but once again, Fletcher fails to keep his word, then lies to cover up the real reason he didn't make it. His ex-wife, Audrey, has had enough and decides to leave town with Max. As Max blows out the candles on his birthday cake, he says, "I wish, for just one day, Dad couldn't tell a lie."

Miraculously, Max's wish comes true. For a full twenty-four hours, Fletcher is unable to tell a lie. He cannot even conceal the truth. This leads to a series of hilarious, embarrassing—and, to tell the truth, sometimes profane—situations. It also spells disaster for Fletcher's career, since he's representing a client, Samantha Cole, who is fighting for custody of her children. Her chief witness is willing to lie to help Samantha win, but Fletcher can't even question a witness if he knows the answer will be a lie.

Amazingly, Fletcher manages to win the case by finding an obscure loophole in the law, and Samantha takes her children away. Fletcher then remembers that his own ex-wife, Audrey, is about to leave town with Max, and realizing what is truly important in life, he races to the airport and manages to stop them just in time. Fletcher has found that telling the truth is so liberating that even after the twenty-four-hour period is over, he determines to continue being honest.

During the court case, Fletcher shouted out, "And the truth shall set you free!" He was quoting Jesus Christ, who said, "You will know the truth, and the truth will set you free" (John 8:32 NIV). This works on two levels: learning the truth about Jesus—that He is God's Son and only He can save us—sets us free from sin and death; and speaking the truth and refusing to lie is very personally liberating.

As Christians, we are to always tell the truth. Lying is wrong. This does not mean, however, that we should be tactlessly blunt, like Fletcher was to his co-workers and even to total strangers. Christians are not only to be known for their honesty, but for "speaking the truth in love" (Ephesians 4:15 NKJV).

*Therefore, putting away lying, "Let every one
of you speak truth with his neighbor,"
for we are members of one another.*
EPHESIANS 4:25 NKJV

 **TAKE TWO**

Have you ever told one little white lie that turned
into a giant snowball of deception? What were the
consequences? Did you find yourself eventually
owning up to the truth and wishing you hadn't lied
in the first place?

Was there ever an instance it was difficult to tell the
truth because it made you unpopular? Did knowing
that we're to be God-pleasers, rather than people-
pleasers, make the situation more bearable?

I've seen this movie ❏

My Star Review ☆ ☆ ☆ ☆ ☆

LIFE IS BEAUTIFUL

Rated: PG-13

Released October 23, 1998

Written by Vincenzo Cerami and Roberto Benigni

Directed by Roberto Benigni

Distributed by Miramax Films

Starring:

Roberto Benigni (Guido Orefice)

Nicoletta Braschi (Dora)

Giorgio Cantarini (Joshua Orefice)

Giustino Durano (Eliseo Orefice)

Sergio Bini Bustric (Ferruccio Papini)

Marisa Paredes (Madre di Dora)

EYES ON THE PRIZE

*L**ife Is Beautiful* is a powerful Italian film that embeds intense themes of valor amid death in actor/director Roberto Benigni's over-the-top energy and humor.

The story is divided into two major acts. The first part is a comedy-romance covering Guido's hilarious courtship and marriage to Dora and their early family life with their young son, Joshua. In the second act, the family ends up in a Nazi concentration camp. To shield Joshua from the horror, Guido convinces him they are part of a grand game in competition for a prize tank. The goal is to reach one-thousand points by hiding from the guards, remaining quiet, and not crying. Guido is able to maintain this imaginative and lighthearted alternative world for Joshua until the American liberators finally arrive. Sadly, Guido must ultimately give his life to save his son from the horror and the retreating but no less vengeful Nazi guards. Yet to the very end, Guido still acts as if "life is beautiful" to ensure that it will be for his firstborn.

Watching this film, we witness the power of the prophetic imagination that overcomes despair by declaring and living an alternative vision—not the plain denial of reality, but a stubborn will to transcend the gray promise of death. By keeping our eyes on the prize and actually living above death and despair, the conditions are created by which a beautiful life can sprout, blossom, and bear fruit.

This is exactly what the Old Testament prophets are up to when they pronounce their visions of streams in the desert, the banqueting table of Mount Zion, and the open gates of New Jerusalem to homesick exiles by the rivers of Babylon. They proclaim hope for renewal that empowers the hopeless to lift up their eyes, waiting in expectancy for the Messiah, and live *today* as free children of God, right under the noses of their captors.

While the prophetic imagination sustains persecuted and impoverished believers around the world, many of us who live more comfortably may not recognize such visions as more than wishful thinking. The New Testament asks more of us. By setting our minds on what is true, noble, right, pure, lovely, admirable, excellent, and praiseworthy (see Philippians 4:8), we become agents who cause God's kingdom to come and His will to be done, on earth as it is in heaven.

Set your hearts on things above, where Christ is seated at the right hand of God. Set your minds on things above, not on earthly things. For you died, and your life is now hidden with Christ in God.
COLOSSIANS 3:1–3 NIV

TAKE TWO

Although you most likely haven't had to endure anything as horrifying as a concentration camp, you've probably still had to endure some trying circumstances. How did God sustain you during this time?

How can you share God's "prophetic imagination" with the people around you this week, showing them that life is beautiful despite their circumstances?

I've seen this movie ❏

My Star Review ☆ ☆ ☆ ☆ ☆

THE LION KING

Rated: G

Released June 24, 1994

Written by Irene Mecchi, Jonathan Roberts, and
  Linda Woolverton

Directed by Roger Allers and Rob Minkoff

Distributed by Buena Vista

Starring (voices):

Jonathan Taylor Thomas (young Simba)

Matthew Broderick (adult Simba)

Jeremy Irons (Scar)

James Earl Jones (Mufasa)

Moira Kelly (adult Nala)

Nathan Lane (Timon)

Ernie Sabella (Pumbaa)

Robert Guillaume (Rafiki)

Rowan Atkinson (Zazu)

CLAIMING YOUR RIGHTFUL PLACE

The setting of this animated children's movie was inspired by the Serengeti Park where the majestic lion, Mufasa, is king of the Pride Lands and his new-born son, Simba, has just been presented as his heir. Scar, Mufasa's younger brother, *was* next in line and is now very bitter that a "little fur-ball" has displaced him.

Determined to be king, Scar forms an alliance with the hated hyenas, promising that if they help him become king, they'll "never go hungry again." Scar leads Simba down into a gorge, has the hyenas start a wildebeest stampede, then tells Mufasa that Simba is down there. Mufasa heroically rescues Simba, but he himself is killed. Scar then convinces Simba that it's *his* fault his father died and suggests he run away. Simba barely escapes the hyenas' jaws and flees to a distant land.

There Simba befriends a meerkat named Timon and a warthog named Pumbaa. When Timon learns that Simba is an outcast he advises, "When the world turns its back on you, you turn your back on the world." Simba follows this self-serving advice and lives in exile. When he is fully grown, his childhood friend Nala arrives telling him how bad things are under Scar's reign, and begs Simba to return. At first Simba refuses, but encouraged by the mandrill, Rafiki, he goes back, faces his past, defeats Scar, and takes his rightful place as king.

Moses was raised in the Egyptian royal court, but when he grew up, he learned that he was a Hebrew and tried to deliver his people. In his haste, however, he killed an Egyptian taskmaster and, fearing Pharaoh's retribution, fled to a distant land, where he lived in exile. When God called him to return to Egypt, Moses repeatedly protested that he was not equal to the task—but with God's help, he was! (See Exodus 2:1–4:17; 12:40–41.)

Like Simba and Moses, many of us once believed God had great plans for our life, but have since become convinced that our mistakes and sins have disqualified us—that we are no longer worthy of such a high calling. We need to realize that God has forgiven our past and still has a place for us in His kingdom.

*Neither fornicators, nor idolaters, nor adulterers,
nor effeminate ... nor thieves, nor covetous, nor
drunkards, nor revilers, nor extortioners, shall inherit
the kingdom of God. And such were some of you:
but ye are washed, but ye are sanctified, but ye are
justified in the name of the Lord Jesus.*
1 CORINTHIANS 6:9–11 KJV

 **TAKE TWO**

Do you feel unworthy to meet the challenges of your
calling from God? What can you do to change that
attitude?

Although you may have confessed your sins to God
and received His forgiveness, have you forgiven
yourself? If not, do so today and walk forward in the
strength of God's Spirit that lives within you!

I've seen this movie ❑

My Star Review ☆ ☆ ☆ ☆ ☆

THE LORD OF THE RINGS
THE FELLOWSHIP OF THE RING

Rated: PG-13

Released December 19, 2001

Written by Fran Walsh, Philippa Boyens, and Peter Jackson

Based upon the novel *The Fellowship of the Ring* by J. R. R. Tolkien

Directed by Peter Jackson

Distributed by New Line Cinema

Starring:

Ian Holm (Bilbo Baggins)

Elijah Wood (Frodo Baggins)

Sean Astin (Samwise Gamgee)

Dominic Monaghan (Meriadoc "Merry" Brandybuck)

Billy Boyd (Peregrin "Pippin" Took)

Ian McKellen (Gandalf)

Viggo Mortensen (Strider/Aragorn)

John Rhys-Davies (Gimli)

Orlando Bloom (Legolas)

Sean Bean (Boromir)

Cate Blanchett (Galadriel)

THE MOST UNLIKELY IMAGINABLE

In the last, dying days of the Third Age, an ancient, evil power named Sauron arises in the land of Mordor and begins amassing armies of Orcs, intent on conquering all Middle Earth. Sauron, terrifying as he is, had once been more powerful, but he had imbued the One Ring with much of his power—and then that ring had been lost. Sauron desperately seeks it to regain his former power.

As Galadriel explains, the Ring had been found "by the most unlikely creature imaginable," Bilbo Baggins, a Hobbit, who has left the ring to his nephew, Frodo. Pursued by Ringwraiths, Frodo and three other Hobbits flee to the elvish stronghold of Rivendell, where a council of Elves, Dwarves, and Men gathers to discuss what to do with the ring.

Gandalf says, "It is in Men that we must place our hope." "Men?" Elrond retorts. "Men are weak!" And of all the races of Men, the weakest and smallest are the Hobbits, barely over three feet tall. Yet when none else dares, Frodo volunteers to carry the ring into the heart of Mordor and destroy it in the fires of Mount Doom, where it was forged.

Saruman expresses the opinion of many when he says, "You did not seriously think that a Hobbit could contend with the will of Sauron! There are none that can!" Yet it is indeed a Hobbit, Frodo, who will find the strength and courage within himself to destroy the ring and bring down Sauron's empire.

When the angel of the Lord told Gideon, "Go in this might of yours, and you shall save Israel from the hand of the Midianites," Gideon replied, "O my Lord, how can I save Israel? Indeed my clan is the weakest in Manasseh, and I am the least in my father's house" (Judges 6:14–15 NKJV). Yet Gideon did deliver Israel!

Like Gideon and Frodo, we may have thought too long and hard upon our own weaknesses and inabilities, or been swayed by others to believe we can never accomplish anything of worth. Yet it is often the weak and despised people God chooses to be heroes. We just have to be willing to accept the task and have the faith that God will help us.

*God has chosen the foolish things of the world to
put to shame the wise, and God has chosen the
weak things of the world to put to shame
the things which are mighty. . .and the things
which are despised God has chosen.*
1 CORINTHIANS 1:27–28 NKJV

TAKE TWO

With only five smooth stones, David succeeded in
killing a giant. Do you believe you, like David, can do
the impossible with seemingly weak weapons? If not,
how can you change that attitude?

Do you have discouragers in your life, people who tell
you you'll never achieve anything worthwhile? What
can you do to drown out those voices and open your
ears to God's?

I've seen this movie ❏

My Star Review ☆ ☆ ☆ ☆ ☆

MINORITY REPORT

Rated: PG-13

Released June 21, 2002

Written by Scott Frank and Jon Cohen

Based on a short story by Philip K. Dick

Directed by Steven Spielberg

Distributed by 20th Century Fox

Starring:

Tom Cruise (Chief John Anderton)

Colin Farrell (Danny Witwer)

Max Von Sydow (Director Lamar Burgess)

Steve Harris (Jad)

Neal McDonough (Fletcher)

Jessica Capshaw (Evanna)

"YOU CAN CHOOSE!"

The year is 2054. John Anderton heads "Pre-crime," a specialized police force in Washington, DC, charged with identifying and arresting murderers *before* they commit their crimes. Pre-crime is able to do this through the powers of three "Pre-cogs"—genetically altered individuals who can see into the future and determine the names of the victim, the killer, and the time and date of the crime. The police piece the rest of the details together by studying the Pre-cogs' visions.

Anderton, whose son was kidnapped years ago, thinks the system is perfect—until the Pre-cogs predict Anderton will murder a complete stranger within the next thirty-six hours. Believing he's been set up, Anderton flees, a fugitive from the very system he helped to perfect. Now he must prove the vision false or figure out a way to stop himself from committing the crime before it's too late.

Anderton's initial doubts about the reliability of the Pre-crime system are confirmed when he finds a "minority report" detailing a situation where one of the Pre-cogs saw something different from the others. For the first time, Anderton starts to believe that maybe the future isn't predetermined after all. As the dissenting Pre-cog, Agatha, keeps telling Anderton, "You can choose!" And choose he does. After working for six years to help build the Pre-crime system, Anderton now decides to tear it down.

In the process, not only does he clear his name, he also exposes the people trying to frame him. As a result, the Pre-crime system is closed down, everyone convicted under the system released, and the Pre-cogs taken to a secret location where they can live out the rest of their days in peace. Anderton is also reunited with his estranged wife, Lara, who is pregnant with another child. Perhaps their future isn't predetermined after all.

At the heart of *Minority Report* is the age-old question of destiny versus free will. Do we really have the power to choose the direction our lives will take, or is our future predetermined? While there has been much debate about this topic in different Christian circles, verses like James 4:17 ("Anyone, then, who knows the good he ought to do and doesn't do it, sins" [NIV]) make it abundantly clear that the power to do good or evil is literally in our hands. This is a tremendous responsibility but also an incredible gift. God has released us to be His agents of grace in the world. So don't let your past determine your future. Remember that, like Anderton, you can choose!

> *So if the Son sets you free,*
> *you will be free indeed.*
> JOHN 8:36 NIV

 **TAKE TWO**

Have you ever felt trapped by the consequences of your past mistakes? What decisions can you make today to help create a better future for you and your loved ones?

Do you know someone who feels anxious about the future? What can you do to help assure that person that he or she has nothing to fear?

I've seen this movie ❏

My Star Review ☆ ☆ ☆ ☆ ☆

MY BIG FAT GREEK WEDDING

Rated: PG

Released April 19, 2002

Written by Nia Vardalos

Directed by Joel Zwick

Distributed by Warner Bros.

Starring:

Nia Vardalos (Fotoula "Toula" Portokalos)

John Corbett (Ian Miller)

Michael Constantine (Kostas "Gus" Portokalos)

Lainie Kazan (Maria Portokalos)

Andrea Martin (Aunt Voula)

Stavroula Logothettis (Athena Portokalos)

Louis Mandylor (Nick Portokalos)

Gia Carides (Cousin Nikki)

ONE BIG FAMILY

In this romantic comedy, Toula Portokalos is a thirty-year-old single Greek woman whose parents are pressuring her to marry. Of course, since they are very conservative Greeks and intensely proud of their heritage, the groom has to be Greek. None of the suitors they bring to their daughter appeal to her, however. Toula feels doomed. She says, "Nice Greek girls who don't find a husband work in the family restaurant. So here I am, day after day, year after year, thirty and way past my expiration date."

In addition to running the family restaurant, Dancing Zorba's, Toula feels suffocated by her large, extended family and her all-compassing culture. She laments that she was forced to go to Greek school and that she was so different from other girls her age. In a bid to escape her restaurant job and her culture, Toula takes computer classes at college so she can work in her aunt's travel agency.

In the process, Toula meets a man named Ian Miller and the two fall in love. There's only one problem. Ian is not Greek. He's *xenos*—a foreigner. Actually, there are several problems, but that's the biggest one. Toula and Ian encounter several comedic impasses as she seeks to get her family to accept him. Gus Portokalos (Toula's father) at first stubbornly says, "No!" when Ian asks to date his daughter, but eventually relents as Ian learns Greek customs and even converts to the Greek Orthodox church.

Gus insists, "There are two kinds of people—Greeks, and everyone else who wish they was Greek." In New Testament times, it was the other way around. Though many Jewish Christians were happy that Greeks were becoming Christians, others insisted that Greeks had to undergo Jewish rites and convert to Judaism first to be saved (see Acts 11:20–23; 15:1, 5). Thankfully, the Christian leaders stopped that.

Even today, we as Christians often smugly believe in the superiority of our own church and look down upon Christians of other denominations. Yet as Paul said, in God's eyes there's no difference between believers, and people "from every nation, from all tribes and peoples" will be in heaven (Revelation 7:9 RSV). As long as others are sincere Christians, let's accept them!

*There is neither Jew nor Greek, slave nor free, male
nor female, for you are all one in Christ Jesus.*
GALATIANS 3:28 NIV

 **TAKE TWO**

Do you feel uncomfortable when you attend worship
services or weddings at churches outside your
denomination? How can you be more accepting of
the different ways Christians worship God?

Does your church worship with contemporary,
traditional, or a blend of these two styles of music?
Do you look down on others who don't share your
taste in worship music? If so, why? And how can you
change that attitude for the better?

I've seen this movie ❑

My Star Review ☆ ☆ ☆ ☆ ☆

NATIONAL TREASURE

Rated: PG

Released November 19, 2004

Written by Jim Kouf, Oren Aviv, and Charles Segars

Story by Jim Kouf, Marianne Wibberley, and Cormac Wibberley

Directed by Jon Turteltaub

Distributed by Buena Vista International

Starring:

Nicolas Cage (Ben Gates)

Hunter Gomez (young Ben Gates)

Christopher Plummer (John Adams Gates)

Jon Voight (Patrick Gates)

Justin Bartha (Riley Poole)

Diane Kruger (Abigail Chase)

Sean Bean (Ian Howe)

Harvey Keitel (FBI agent Peter Sadusky)

David Dayan Fisher (Shaw)

"YOU'RE TREASURE HUNTERS,
AREN'T YOU?"

As young Ben Gates listens, his grandfather explains their family's history as treasure hunters: The Knights Templar had discovered the treasures of the ages and transported them to the United States just before the Revolutionary War. There they formed the Freemasons—several of whom were Founding Fathers—hid the treasure from the British, then created a series of clues leading to it. In 1832, the last surviving signer of the Declaration of Independence told Thomas Gates (their ancestor) a clue.

As an adult, Ben Gates, together with his friend Riley Poole and financial backer Ian Howe, follows the clue to the *Charlotte*, a ship bound in the polar ice, and there Ben finds a pipe containing a startling message: The treasure map is on the Declaration of Independence! Ben is unwilling to tamper with such a priceless document, but Ian disagrees, and the two part ways—explosively.

Ben warns the FBI that Ian intends to steal the

Declaration, but they disbelieve him, confident that it's too heavily guarded, so Ben decides that the only way to protect the document is to steal it himself. In the process, Abigail Chase, the Declaration's guardian, becomes mixed up in his misadventures. Now Ian's men and the FBI (led by Agent Sadusky) are in hot pursuit of Ben, Riley, and Abigail as they find one clue after another.

Finally, Ben and his father Patrick lead the way to the immense treasure trove in a chamber deep beneath Trinity Church. In a happy ending, Ben and Abigail end up fabulously rich after accepting a mere 1 percent of the treasure as a finder's fee.

King Solomon was the richest ruler in the ancient world, and the Bible tells us that "every year King Solomon received over twenty-five tons of gold" (1 Kings 10:14 GNT). Treasure hunters insist that the source of Solomon's gold was a mine in Ophir (see 1 Kings 9:26–28) somewhere in Arabia, Africa, or India—but they've never found it.

Solomon was also a very *wise* man, and millions down through the ages have been enriched by reading his inspired writings. And guess what? Solomon tells us it's cool to search for treasure—adding that we should search for wisdom and knowledge with the same dedication and intensity. Clue: We can find these spiritual treasures in the pages of the Bible.

Listen to what is wise and try to understand it.
Yes, beg for knowledge; plead for insight.
Look for it as hard as you would for silver
or some hidden treasure.
PROVERBS 2:2–4 GNT

TAKE TWO

Do you make it a point to study the wise adages found in Proverbs? If and when you do, how would your life change if you made an effort to not only study Solomon's sayings but *apply* them to your life?

Jesus is our spiritual treasure. How much time do you spend seeking His wisdom? Or asking the Holy Spirit to help you find the message of His Word?

I've seen this movie ❑

My Star Review ☆ ☆ ☆ ☆ ☆

NORTH BY NORTHWEST

Rated: Unrated
Released July 17, 1959
Written by Ernest Lehman
Directed by Alfred Hitchcock
Distributed by Metro-Goldwyn-Mayer

Starring:

Cary Grant (Roger O. Thornhill)
Eva Marie Saint (Eve Kendall)
James Mason (Phillip Vandamm)
Jessie Royce Landis (Clara Thornhill)
Leo G. Carroll (the Professor)
Philip Ober (Lester Townsend)
Adam Williams (Valerian)
Robert Ellenstein (Licht)
Martin Landau (Leonard)

A CASE OF MISTAKEN IDENTITY

It's the height of the Cold War and the United States wants to arrest Philip Vandamm for selling classified secrets to the enemy, so when a government agency led by the "Professor" discovers that Eve Kendall has become romantically involved with Vandamm, they persuade her to become their informant. Vandamm is suspicious that he's under surveillance, however, so the agency creates a fictitious agent named Kaplan to draw Vandamm's attention away from Eve.

Things take a twist when Vandamm's henchmen, Valerian and Licht, attempt to flush out the nonexistent Kaplan and mistake advertising executive Roger Thornhill—who up till now has lead "a dull life"—for the spy. They kidnap Thornhill and take him to a mountaintop estate where they get him drunk so he'll talk, but when he insists that he knows nothing, they put him behind the wheel of a car to push him over a cliff to his death.

Thornhill breaks free and survives a careening ride down the mountain road, then finds himself running for his life, accused of being "a dangerous assassin. . . a mad killer," with no idea of why people are after him. Eventually, however, he meets the Professor who clues him in. Things become even more complicated when Thornhill crosses paths with Eve Kendall and his actions cause Vandamm's men to suspect Eve. Thornhill must now risk his life to rescue her—which, after a harrowing adventure, he does.

Paul once ended up in huge trouble when he was in Jerusalem and mistaken for somebody else: First, his religious enemies accused him of being "the man" who went everywhere blaspheming the temple and their faith. To make matters worse, the Roman tribune who arrested Paul mistook him for an Egyptian criminal mastermind, the leader of four thousand assassins who had recently started a revolt (see Acts 21:27–39).

Like Paul, we're sometimes mistaken for troublemakers when all we're trying to do is share the gospel with others and live a godly life. This can cause misunderstandings and persecution. We're told to pray "that we may lead a quiet and peaceable life in all godliness and dignity" (1 Timothy 2:2 RSV), but are warned that we'll occasionally experience unwanted excitement in the form of persecution. So don't be surprised!

*Now you have observed. . .the things that happened
to me at Antioch, at Iconium, and Lystra. What
persecutions I endured! Yet the Lord rescued me
from all of them. Indeed, all who want to live a godly
life in Christ Jesus will be persecuted.*
2 Timothy 3:10–12 RSV

◼ TAKE TWO

Have you ever faced persecution because of your
Christian beliefs? Did you respond with godliness and
dignity?

Do you know of any missionaries who face or have
faced persecution? What have they suffered? How
can you ease their burden?

I've seen this movie ❑

My Star Review ☆ ☆ ☆ ☆ ☆

THE PASSION OF THE CHRIST

Rated: R

Released February 25, 2004

Written by Benedict Fitzgerald and Mel Gibson

Directed by Mel Gibson

Distributed by 20th Century Fox

Starring:

James Caviezel (Jesus)

Maia Morgenstern (Mary)

Christo Jivkov (John)

Francesco De Vito (Peter)

Monica Bellucci (Mary Magdalene)

Mattia Sbragia (Caiphas)

Toni Bertorelli (Annas)

Luca Lionello (Judas)

Hristo Shopov (Pontius Pilate)

THE ULTIMATE SACRIFICE

In the dramatic movie *The Passion of the Christ*, Mel Gibson sets an age-old story in an entirely new light. The movie's main focus is the last twelve hours of Jesus' life, from His arrest to His crucifixion, yet although Christians are very familiar with these events, this movie depicts them with vivid realism. For one thing, the actors speak entirely in Latin, Greek, and Aramaic; the only English is in the subtitles.

In *The Passion of the Christ*, Jesus is a controversial miracle-worker and teacher who has attracted a large following of Jews throughout the Roman provinces of Judea and Galilee, but has also galvanized most of the Sanhedrin (the ruling Jewish council) against Him because He claims to be the Messiah, the King of the Jews. This is a dangerous claim. Not only do the members of the Sanhedrin disbelieve Him, but they're afraid Jesus will bring the wrath of the Romans down upon them.

They therefore bribe one of Jesus' disciples, Judas Iscariot, to betray Him and lead soldiers to where He's praying in the Garden of Gethsemane. The guards arrest Jesus and take Him to the high priest's house, where they try Him for blasphemy; then they take Him to Pilate, the Roman governor, to be crucified. Pilate tries to appease them by having Jesus flogged with a cat-o'-nine-tails instead, but in the end, gives in to the mob and orders Jesus to be crucified.

The movie is rated R for the amount of raw violence it portrays, and the graphic scenes of Christ being beaten and whipped do indeed shock the senses. And our senses *need* to be shocked. We read in the Bible that the Roman soldiers "scourged" Jesus and put "a crown of thorns" on his head (Matthew 27:26, 29 NKJV), but we're detached from what this really means. *The Passion of the Christ* doesn't allow us to ignore how much Christ suffered for us.

Gibson said, "This is a movie about love, hope, faith, and forgiveness. He died for all mankind, suffered for all of us. It's time to get back to that basic message." If this movie achieves no other goal than to make us thankful for the terrible price Jesus paid for our salvation, then it has already accomplished a great deal.

He was pierced for our transgressions,
he was crushed for our iniquities;
the punishment that brought us peace was upon
him, and by his wounds we are healed.
ISAIAH 53:5 NIV

 **TAKE TWO**

Thinking back on Christ's crucifixion, are you amazed
He remained silent during such agony and made
no move to strike out against His aggressors? Is His
gentleness, His submissiveness a quality you'd like to
emulate?

Jesus asked God to forgive those who persecuted
Him. Is there someone you need to forgive—as Christ
forgave us as well as His persecutors?

I've seen this movie ❏

My Star Review ☆ ☆ ☆ ☆ ☆

PIRATES *of the* CARIBBEAN
THE CURSE OF THE BLACK PEARL

Rated: PG-13

Released July 9, 2003

Written by Ted Elliot, Terry Rossio, Stuart Beattie, and Jay Wolpert

Directed by Gore Verbinski

Distributed by Walt Disney Pictures

Starring:

Johnny Depp (Captain Jack Sparrow)

Geoffrey Rush (Hector Barbossa)

Orlando Bloom (Will Turner)

Keira Knightley (Elizabeth Swann)

Jack Davenport (Commodore James Norrington)

Mackenzie Crook (Ragetti)

WHERE DO YOU
STORE YOUR TREASURE?

In *Pirates of the Caribbean: The Curse of the Black Pearl*, a rum-loving pirate, Jack Sparrow, and a young blacksmith/swordsman, Will Turner, chase down the *Black Pearl*, a fabled pirate ship captained by the evil, living-dead Hector Barbossa. Sparrow's covetous eye is on the *Black Pearl* and treasure. Turner, meanwhile, is focused on rescuing the pirates' hostage, the beautiful Elizabeth Swann.

The backstory of the *Black Pearl* is that her crew had plundered and squandered a treasure chest full of cursed gold medallions. The sailors are now under a spell of immortality, appearing as ghastly skeletons under the moonlight. Barbossa's obsession is to break the curse by tracking down each of the coins and returning them to the chest, along with a drop of blood from each of his pirates. The final medallion came from one of Captain Barbossa's original shipmates, Bootstrap Bill Turner—Will's father. But it's now in Elizabeth's possession.

Deceived into thinking Elizabeth is Bootstrap Bill's daughter, Barbossa sails with her for the Isla de Muerta to finish the job. Will and Sparrow are in hot pursuit, with the double-crossing Norrington (who's in love with Elizabeth) not far behind.

Jack Sparrow's elusive motives and unpredictable allegiance come to a head in an exciting battle in and around the treasure trove of de Muerta. By all accounts, the comically eccentric Jack Sparrow steals the show by continually keeping us guessing as to whether his hedonism or heroism will get the last word.

As in this movie, treasure also plays a part in the trials or downfall of a number of biblical characters. Joseph hid some treasure in his brothers' sacks to entrap Benjamin (see Genesis 44). Achan's buried treasure led to Israel's defeat at Ai and to his entire family's death (see Joshua 7). Hezekiah lost his kingdom after revealing all of his treasures to envoys from Babylon (see 2 Kings 20). Subsequently, the people of God began to gather wisdom about true and false treasures, collecting proverbs on the topic in Solomon's famous books. For example, we read, "Ill-gotten treasures are of no value, but righteousness delivers from death" (Proverbs 10:2 NIV).

Jesus also exhorts us not to obsess about earthly treasures or hoarding wealth, which are fleeting and temporal, but to invest in that kingdom that is eternal. Sowing seeds of love and compassion, faith and faithfulness, and treasuring wisdom and revelation—these are virtues that deposit savings and reap blessings beyond the grave.

But store up for yourselves treasures in heaven, where moth and rust do not destroy, and where thieves do not break in and steal. For where your treasure is, there your heart will be also.
MATTHEW 6:20–21 NIV

 **TAKE TWO**

Have you ever been tripped up by treasure? What steps can you take to avoid similar incidents in the future?

Like Jack Sparrow, we're often unsure of our own motives up until the last moment. Think of something you're pursuing right now. What are your motives for going after it?

I've seen this movie ❑

My Star Review ✰ ✰ ✰ ✰ ✰

THE POSEIDON ADVENTURE

Rated: PG

Released December 13, 1972

Written by Wendell Mayes and Stirling Silliphant

Based on a novel by Paul Gallico

Directed by Ronald Neame and Irwin Allen

Distributed by 20th Century Fox

Starring:

Gene Hackman (Rev. Frank Scott)

Ernest Borgnine (Det. Lt. Mike Rogo)

Red Buttons (James Martin)

Roddy McDowell (Acres)

Shelley Winters (Belle Rosen)

Jack Albertson (Manny Rosen)

Pamela Sue Martin (Susan Shelby)

Eric Shea (Robin Shelby)

LIFESAVING 101

In the 1972 thriller *The Poseidon Adventure,* Gene Hackman portrays an unorthodox preacher who believes God only helps those who help themselves. As the Reverend Frank Scott, he puts his philosophy into practice when a New Year's Eve tidal wave capsizes the cruise ship he's on.

In a surreal, topsy-turvy environment—passengers walk on ceilings while tables and chairs, bolted to the floors, hang above their heads—Hackman leads a diverse group of survivors on a perilous journey to the hull of the ship. Convinced that the only way out is to move toward the ship's *bottom*, now above water, Hackman argues with the SS *Poseidon*'s purser, who urges other passengers to stay where they are and await rescue.

Frustrated, Hackman guides his team of eight—a young boy and his teenage sister, a crusty cop and his sharp-tongued wife, a retired couple traveling to visit their grandson, a pleasant bachelor haberdasher, and an eager-to-please ship's steward—out of the ship's grand ballroom. They use a large, artificial Christmas tree to climb from the ballroom ceiling to the kitchen entrance, now some thirty feet above.

His group safely in the kitchen hallway, Hackman calls down to the purser and his passengers, urging them once more to join the journey to the hull. They all refuse—until seawater breaches the ballroom level and the passengers panic. Many rush the Christmas tree, desperately trying to climb up as Hackman urges calm. But with so many people hanging off the tree, it falls backward into the swirling water. Hackman watches in dismay, then reluctantly turns away, knowing the entire group will be lost.

It's hard to avoid a comparison with Noah. Though the hero of Genesis 6–9 would have had a different view of God than *The Poseidon Adventure*'s Reverend Scott, both Noah and the movie preacher called others—unsuccessfully—to salvation from raging waters.

Noah was both "a righteous man" (Genesis 6:9 NIV) and "a preacher of righteousness" (2 Peter 2:5 NIV). By his example and his words, he showed the people of his day the way of life.

Today, we have the same calling and privilege. Though others won't always listen to us, we should be sharing—in whatever ways possible—the life-giving truth of the gospel.

*"Those who are wise will shine like the brightness
of the heavens, and those who lead many to
righteousness, like the stars for ever and ever."*
Daniel 12:3 NIV

TAKE TWO

When was the last time you shared the gospel
message with a pre-Christian? Where is that person
now? Has that individual found his or her way to
Christ? Perhaps it's time to follow up.

One of the best ways to introduce someone to Jesus
is by sharing His love. Who in your life needs that
love the most? Who is the most willing to receive it?

I've seen this movie ❏

My Star Review ☆ ☆ ☆ ☆ ☆

THE PRINCESS BRIDE

Rated: PG

Released September 25, 1987

Written by William Golman

Based on the novel by William Golman

Directed by Rob Reiner

Distributed by 20th Century Fox

Starring:

Fred Savage (the Grandson)

Peter Falk (the Grandfather/Narrator)

Robin Wright (Buttercup)

Cary Elwes (Westley)

Mandy Patinkin (Inigo Montoya)

André the Giant (Fezzik)

Wallace Shawn (Vizzini)

Christopher Guest (Count Tyrone Rugen)

Chris Sarandon (Prince Humperdinck)

Billy Crystal (Miracle Max)

"AS YOU WISH"

Buttercup lives on a farm in the land of Florin, and whenever she gives her farmhand Westley an order, he replies, "As you wish." When she realizes that "as you wish" means "I love you," Buttercup confesses her love for Westley as well. Soon he goes forth to make his fortune so they can marry. After he's been gone five years, however, Buttercup hears he's been captured by ruthless pirates. Assuming he's dead, she reluctantly agrees to marry Prince Humperdinck, the ruler of Florin.

Just before their marriage, three outlaws kidnap Buttercup: Vizzini, a Sicilian criminal mastermind; the Turkish giant Fezzik; and the Spanish swordsman, Inigo Montoya—who is seeking revenge on the six-fingered man who killed his father. Humperdinck and his men pursue the trio, but a masked man in black catches up to them first. After defeating the three outlaws, the masked man reveals to Buttercup that he's Westley.

After a skirt-scorching stroll through the Fire Swamp, Buttercup and Westley are captured by

Prince Humperdinck. Agreeing to release Westley, Humperdinck rides off with Buttercup, leaving Westley in the hands of Humperdinck's henchman, Count Rugen, who later tortures Westley to death in the Pit of Despair.

When Montoya learns Rugen is the man who killed his father, he and Fezzik find the "almost dead" Westley and take him to the magician, Miracle Max, who brings him back to life. Montoya then kills Count Rugen and the three friends rescue Buttercup, who is about to marry the prince. The ceremony is cut short before she says "I do," so she is free to marry Westley.

Westley chides Buttercup, "I told you I would always come for you. Why didn't you wait for me?" Buttercup replies, "Well, you were dead." Westley responds, "Death cannot stop true love." The love between Westley and Buttercup has strong parallels to the love of Christ for the Church. Like Westley, Jesus was tortured to death, then brought back to life, and will one day marry His bride (see 2 Corinthians 11:2; Revelation 19:7–8).

Jesus has proved His love for us; now we must prove our love for Him. Jesus said, "Greater love hath no man than this, that a man lay down his life for his friends. Ye are my friends, if ye do whatsoever I command you" (John 15:13–14 KJV). Loving Jesus means saying "As you wish" to whatsoever He wishes.

If ye love me, keep my commandments.
JOHN 14:15 KJV

 **TAKE TWO**

In one scene Buttercup tells Humperdinck, "You can't hurt me. Westley and I are joined by the bonds of love." Is your bond with Jesus so strong that others can't truly hurt you? If not, how can you fortify that bond?

When Westley went off to seek his fortune, Buttercup, in a sense, lost faith in his ever returning. Do you have faith that Christ will return? Fortunately, He left you His love letter—the Bible—to dispel any doubt or fear. Have you read it lately?

I've seen this movie ❑

My Star Review ☆ ☆ ☆ ☆ ☆

RAIDERS of the *LOST ARK*

Rated: PG

Released June 12, 1981

Written by Lawrence Kasdan

Based on a story by George Lucas and Philip
  Kaufman

Directed by Steven Spielberg

Distributed by Paramount Pictures

Starring:

Harrison Ford (Indiana Jones)

Karen Allen (Marion)

Paul Freeman (Belloq)

Ronald Lacey (Toht)

John Rhys-Davies (Sallah)

Denholm Elliott (Brody)

THE ULTIMATE QUEST

In this adventure film, Indiana Jones, one of cinema's most iconic characters, goes after the ultimate artifact—the lost Ark of the Covenant, the news of which resurfaces when the Nazis discover its presumed final resting place—the ancient Egyptian city of Tanis.

Obsessed with the occult and religious relics, Adolf Hitler has, ironically, set his sights upon this Jewish artifact, thinking it will allow him to access God's power. Bent on stopping Hitler from capturing the Ark, American intelligence agents commission Indiana Jones to locate the Ark and bring it back to America before the Nazis recover it.

Indy's first stop is Nepal, where he hopes to find a key artifact that will allow him to locate the Ark. But the Nazis secretly follow him there, and he barely escapes with his life, the artifact, and his ex-girlfriend, Marion.

Indy and Marion set off for Egypt, where they link up with Indy's old friend Sallah. With Sallah's help, Indy realizes he has an edge, because the Nazis are missing a key piece of information with which he quickly locates the true location of the Ark and starts digging.

Unfortunately, the Nazis—led by Indy's archrival, a French archaeologist named Belloq—show up, seize the Ark, then seal Indy and Marion into the Well of Souls, a snake-infested temple.

Through bravery, resourcefulness, and luck, Indy and Marion escape, and then Indy gets the Ark back from the Nazis in one of the best chase scenes ever filmed. Once again, it looks like Indy, Marion, and the Ark are home free. But Belloq and the Nazis capture Marion and the Ark and take them to a secret submarine base, where Belloq plans to open the Ark during a ritualized ceremony. Marion and Indy are forced to watch as Belloq opens the Ark, unleashing a horrible death upon him and his Nazi companions. Only Indy and Marion, who respect the true power the Ark contains, survive, proving all too well that, "The fear of the LORD is the beginning of wisdom" (Psalm 111:10 NIV).

Like the ancient Israelites and their enemies, Belloq and the Nazis discover that God cannot be confined to a box like some genie to be manipulated into granting our wishes. The same applies to anything we might revere like the Ark today. God will not be boxed or bullied, detained or released by any artifact. He is still far greater than any man-made thing. Therefore, let your greatest quest be for God, not just for the gifts He gives.

*"I love those who love me,
and those who seek me find me."*
PROVERBS 8:17 NIV

 **TAKE TWO**

Have you let your eyes slip away from God and fixed them on something less than Him, no matter how good? Ask God to help you readjust your focus today.

Why do you think the character of Indiana Jones resonates with so many people? In what ways is he like a Christ figure? In what ways is he different?

I've seen this movie ❏

My Star Review ☆ ☆ ☆ ☆ ☆

ROCKY

Rated: PG
Released December 3, 1976
Written by Sylvester Stallone
Directed by John G. Avildson
Distributed by United Artists

Starring:
Sylvester Stallone (Rocky Balboa)
Talia Shire (Adrianna Pennino)
Burt Young (Paulie Pennino)
Carl Weathers (Apollo Creed)
Burgess Meredith (Mickey Goldmill)
Thayer David (Jergens)

FIGHT THE GOOD FIGHT!

ocky, one of the greatest underdog flicks of all time, features Rocky Balboa's "Cinderella" rise from obscurity to stardom.

Balboa starts out as an unknown club fighter from Philadelphia, waiting for his big break. Meanwhile, boxing's world champion, Apollo Creed, is booked to defend his title during America's bicentennial. However, when the top contender cancels due to an injury, Creed decides to book a gimmick replacement fight with a local boxer. Rocky's nickname, "the Italian Stallion," makes for good marketing, so Creed picks him, assuming an easy victory over this "nobody."

As the plot proceeds, Rocky enters into relationships with Adrian (his shy girlfriend), Paulie (her cranky brother), and Mick (his relentless manager). Enduring images of his training (set to an adrenaline-pumping musical score) include punching out sides of frozen beef, drinking glasses of raw eggs, and running up the steps of the Philadelphia Art Museum. The final act features the fifteen-round brawl where Rocky goes the distance with a shocked and shaken Creed. The emotional crescendo sweeps the audience along to the judge's split-decision and a swollen-eyed Rocky hollering his girlfriend's name.

Rags-to-riches stories are always entertaining. Something in us wants to cheer on the underdog and see the human spirit prevail against overwhelming odds.

Of course, our rudimentary example is that of the King of kings. His human beginnings were in the stable at Bethlehem, His toddler years were as a refugee in Egypt, His childhood was spent in the hillbilly village of Nazareth, and His first trade was in blue-collar construction. Not only did Jesus rise from peasantry to challenge religious elite and political rulers, He took on Satan and death head-to-head. By His resurrection, Christ delivered the knockout blow to humanity's most fearsome bullies and ascended as World Champion. As many have noted, every great story is only great because it emulates the Great Story.

The story of Jesus invites us to do the same. On one hand, we recognize our own weakness and anonymity. Paul reminded the Corinthians that not many of them were smart or strong, wise or wealthy (see 1 Corinthians 1) and that he had come to them with trembling knees and simple words. It was not his greatness but the message of the cross and the power of God that won their hearts (see 1 Corinthians 2). On the other hand, by the grace of God, we are urged to press on to victory (see Philippians 3:14) and assured of a glorified destiny (see Romans 8:30).

> *I have fought the good fight,*
> *I have finished the race,*
> *I have kept the faith.*
> 2 TIMOTHY 4:7 NIV

 **TAKE TWO**

Have you ever been tempted to "disqualify" yourself because you didn't feel worthy to succeed? According to Scripture, what makes us worthy in God's eyes?

Think about God's definition of *success*. How does it differ from how the world often defines success?

I've seen this movie ❏

My Star Review ☆ ☆ ☆ ☆ ☆

SCHINDLER'S LIST

Rated: R

Released December 15, 1993

Written by Steven Zaillian

Based on the book by Thomas Keneally

Directed by Steven Spielberg

Distributed by Universal Pictures

Starring:

Liam Neeson (Oskar Schindler)

Ben Kingsley (Itzhak Stern)

Ralph Fiennes (Amon Göth)

Caroline Goodall (Emilie Schindler)

Jonathan Sagall (Poldek Pfefferberg)

Embeth Davidtz (Helen Hirsch)

Malgoscha Gebel (Wiktoria Klonowska)

Shmuel Levy (Wilek Chilowicz)

SAVING LIVES, ONE BY ONE

Oskar Schindler is a German businessman from Czechoslovakia and a member of the Nazi party, intent on earning profits on the backs of Jewish slave labor. After arriving in Krakow, Poland, he bribes Nazi officials to give him the use of an abandoned factory to make army mess kits. Schindler then persuades Itzhak Stern, a member of the local Jewish Council, to persuade the Jews to raise the needed capital, in return for small benefits. He takes on Stern to handle business matters.

Schindler begins as an opportunist and a callous businessman, but when the Nazi officer Amon Göth sends the SS to clear the Krakow ghetto, shooting scores of Jews, Schindler is touched. The movie then details the awakening of Schindler's conscience and the steps he takes to rescue "his Jews" from death. To keep them from being shipped off to the concentration camp of Auschwitz, Schindler has a list typed up of the 1,100 Jews he wants to spare, and pays Göth for each name on the list. As Stern observes, "This list. . .is an absolute good. The list is life. All around its margins lies the gulf."

Schindler relocates his Jews to Czechoslovakia, and they are still alive when the Germans surrender and the Russian army arrives to liberate the prisoners. Stern knows, however, that he will be branded as a profiteering war criminal, so he leaves. Before he drives off, Stern gives him a ring engraved with a saying from the Jewish Talmud: "Whoever saves one life, saves the world entire," but Schindler, overcome with emotion, laments, "I didn't do enough!"

We may admire Schindler's courage and sacrifice, but that is not enough. Like Schindler, our consciences, too, must be awakened to see the desperate needs of the world around us. While we cannot do everything, and we may feel it is all we can do to make ends meet, God wishes to touch our hearts with others' needs as well. Surely there will be times when we will have the opportunity to be like the Good Samaritan who helped a wounded Jew on the Jericho road (see Luke 10:25–37).

Even if, like Oskar Schindler, we think that what little we can do is not enough, it *is* enough if it helps even one needy person.

Open your mouth for the speechless,
in the cause of all who are appointed to die.
Open your mouth, judge righteously,
and plead the cause of the poor and needy.
PROVERBS 31:8–9 NKJV

◼ TAKE TWO

Whose life—friend or stranger—can you bless today? Ask God to put the name of an acquaintance on your heart or to lead you to a stranger who needs a helping hand. Then bless that person with God's love and your caring heart.

Stern said that Schindler's "list is life." Do you have a list that expresses the life of Christ within you? How can you close the gulf between yourself and those in need?

I've seen this movie ❏

My Star Review ☆ ☆ ☆ ☆ ☆

THE SHAWSHANK REDEMPTION

Rated: R

Released September 23, 1994

Written by Frank Darabont

Based on the novella *Rita Hayworth and the Shawshank Redemption* by Stephen King

Directed by Frank Darabont

Distributed by Columbia Pictures

Starring:

Tim Robbins (Andy Dufresne)

Morgan Freeman (Ellis Boyd "Red" Redding)

Bob Gunton (Warden Norton)

William Sadler (Heywood)

Clancy Brown (Captain Hadley)

Gil Bellows (Tommy)

Mark Rolston (Bogs Diamond)

James Whitmore (Brooks Hatlen)

Larry Brandenburg (Skeet)

THE POWER OF HOPE

Andy Dufresne is a successful, prosperous banker until the day he learns that his wife is having an affair. To add to the injustice, when she and her lover are murdered, Andy is wrongfully accused of committing the crimes and sentenced to life in Maine's harsh Shawshank Prison. There, confinement, boredom, and hard manual labor begin to break him down. Worst of all, a gang of homosexuals called the Sisters routinely beats and molests him.

When Andy learns that a prisoner nicknamed "Red" is adept at smuggling in contraband items, Andy asks Red to get him a rock hammer so that he can enjoy rock collecting. After this, they become close friends. Later, as the inmates watch the film *Gilda* starring Rita Hayworth, Andy asks Red to get him a poster of the beautiful movie star.

One day Andy confides in Red: "There's something inside. . .that they can't get to, that they can't touch. That's yours." When Red asks, "What're you talking about?" Andy replies, "Hope."

Life changes when Andy uses his knowledge of accounting to keep Hadley, the chief prison guard, from being taxed heavily. Afterward, however, Warden Norton forces Andy to use his banking skills to help embezzle money: Norton hires prisoners out as work gangs to local construction companies and road-building crews and has their wages laundered through an account held by a fictitious "Randall Stephens."

Meanwhile, Andy uses his rock hammer to slowly chip away at his prison wall, hiding his work behind the Rita Hayworth poster. In the end, Andy escapes, takes on the identity of Randall Stephens, and flees to Mexico. Red is later released on parole and reunites with him there.

In the Bible, a young man named Joseph was also falsely accused of a crime and sent to prison. He spent many years there and they "hurt his feet with fetters" (Psalm 105:18 NKJV) until one day he, too, was released (see Genesis 39:1–41:16; Psalm 105:17–21). Like Andy Dufresne, Joseph was kept alive by hope—hope that he would one day be free.

Andy said, "Hope is a good thing, maybe the best of things, and no good thing ever dies." Hope *is* a good thing, and while love for God and others is "the *best* of things," hope is one of the three most vital things we can have in this life. Never give up hope!

And now abide faith, hope, love, these three;
but the greatest of these is love.
1 CORINTHIANS 13:13 NKJV

TAKE TWO

Do you have hope in your life right now? If not, what can you do to regain it? If you have hope, what can you do to raise someone else's?

About God, Job said, "Though he slay me, yet will I hope in him (Job 13:15 NIV). Do you have the hope of Job? If not, what can you do to strengthen it?

I've seen this movie ❏

My Star Review ☆ ☆ ☆ ☆ ☆

SHREK

Rated: PG

Released May 18, 2001

Written by Ted Elliot, Terry Rossio, Joe Stillman,
   and Roger S. H. Schulman

Based on the book by William Steig

Directed by Andrew Adamson and Vickey Jenson

Distributed by DreamWorks SKG

Starring (voices):

Mike Myers (Shrek)

Eddie Murphy (Donkey)

Cameron Diaz (Princess Fiona)

John Lithgow (Lord Farquaad)

Vincent Cassel (Monsieur Hood)

Peter Dennis (Ogre Hunter)

STUCK IN A SWAMP

Shrek is an ogre who wants nothing more than to be left alone in his swamp. Then one day his solitude is interrupted by a host of familiar fairy-tale characters—refugees driven from their territory by the nasty Prince Farquaad. Shrek sets off to Farquaad's palace to protest this unwelcome immigration, accompanied by an annoyingly friendly talking donkey named. . .Donkey. They arrive at the castle just in time for a knightly contest, the winner of which will attempt to rescue Princess Fiona, who's held captive by a fire-breathing dragon. When Shrek wins the match, he strikes a bargain with Farquaad: the princess in exchange for his swamp.

Shrek and Donkey save the princess, a feisty beauty whose expectations of her Prince Charming are dashed by the reality of the ogre's manner and appearance. Nevertheless, as they journey back to Farquaad's palace, romantic feelings start to spark between Shrek and Fiona. Unfortunately, Shrek overhears Fiona confiding in Donkey about a curse she is under, and he mistakes her confession to being an ugly ogre as a description of himself. Before they can clear up the misunderstanding, Farquaad scoops up the princess and takes her away to be married. When Donkey finally gets Shrek to listen to the truth, he and Shrek race to the castle, where the spell on Fiona is broken by a kiss from her true love.

One of the film's key themes is the importance of friendship and community, as exemplified in this exchange:

> **Shrek:** "Why are you following me?"
> **Donkey:** (singing) " 'Cause I'm all alone, there's no one here beside me. . . . But you gotta have friends."
> **Shrek:** "Stop singing! Well, it's no wonder you don't have any friends!"
> **Donkey:** "Wow! Only a true friend would be that cruelly honest!"

Donkey's humorous retort actually echoes a number of Solomon's proverbs (see Proverbs 17:17; 18:24; 27:6). Amid warnings about the betrayal that sometimes comes with friendship (see Psalm 41:9; 55:12–14), the Bible often declares the importance of friendship and dangers of isolation (see Ecclesiastes 4:10).

But the greatest blessing of all is to be known as a "friend of God" (James 2:23 NKJV) and of His Son,

Jesus, who said, "You are my friends if you do what I command. I no longer call you servants, because a servant does not know his master's business. Instead, I have called you friends, for everything that I learned from my Father I have made known to you" (John 15:14–15 NIV).

> *The LORD would speak to Moses face to face,*
> *as a man speaks with his friend.*
> EXODUS 33:11 NIV

 TAKE TWO

Have you ever felt like Shrek, stuck in a swamp and not wanting anyone else around? How did you get into that situation? What got you out?

Think of your friends today. Do any of them need to be called out of isolation and into community like Shrek? What role can you play in this process?

I've seen this movie ❑

My Star Review ☆ ☆ ☆ ☆ ☆

signs

Rated: PG-13
Released August 2, 2002
Written by M. Night Shyamalan
Directed by M. Night Shyamalan
Distributed by Touchstone Pictures

Starring:
Mel Gibson (Father Graham Hess)
Joaquin Phoenix (Merrill Hess)
Rory Culkin (Morgan Hess)
Abigail Breslin (Bo Hess)
Cherry Jones (Officer Caroline Paski)
Patricia Kalember (Colleen Hess)
Ted Sutton (SFC Cunningham)

WHAT KIND OF PERSON ARE YOU?

In *Signs* Father Graham Hess, a former Episcopalian minister, lives on a Bucks County farm outside Philadelphia with his two children and younger brother, Merrill. The film begins six months after the tragic death of Graham's wife, and it's obvious his faith has taken a blow as a result of her passing.

But Graham's grieving is interrupted when a crop circle appears in his cornfield. When more crop circles—and eventually alien spaceships—begin showing up all over the world, Graham and his family hole up in their farmhouse. Watching events unfold on TV, they wonder: *Are the aliens hostile or friendly? Is this the end of the world or the threshold of a new beginning for humankind?*

In a pivotal scene, Graham tells Merrill there are two types of people in the world. The first type believes everything happens for a reason. They interpret events like the aliens' arrival as *signs* that a higher power is at work in the universe. The second type believes things "just happen." The universe is ruled by mere chance.

It becomes obvious that Merrill is in the former camp and Graham in the latter.

Graham's cynicism is put to the test when the alien threat turns into a close encounter of the worst kind. Under direct attack, Graham and his family barricade themselves in the basement, where they wait until they hear an announcement on the radio that the spaceships have left Earth.

Elated, they emerge from the cellar, only to encounter a stranded alien in their living room. In a tense scene, Merrill battles the alien while Graham drags his son, Morgan, outside and attempts to save him from an asthma attack. In the end, Merrill kills the alien and Morgan survives. As a result, Graham's faith in God is restored, and he resumes his vocation as a minister.

An old writer's adage says, "In life, one thing happens after another. In fiction, one thing happens *because* of another." In other words, every event in a story has a purpose that will be realized by tale's end. Real life cannot be sewn up so neatly—some things "just happen" without any apparent order or purpose.

However, *Signs* argues that perhaps life and fiction have more in common than this saying suggests. Even though life's events may seem random on the surface, if we truly believe life has an Author, eventually we will come to see that everything makes sense.

We know that in all things God works for the good of those who love him, who have been called according to his purpose.
ROMANS 8:28 NIV

🎬 TAKE TWO

Struggling to find purpose and meaning in your life? Why don't you ask God for a "sign" to help revitalize your faith?

Do you know someone who is having a difficult time making sense of the curveballs life has thrown his or her way? What can you do to help this person understand God truly has our best interests in mind?

I've seen this movie ❑

My Star Review ☆ ☆ ☆ ☆ ☆

THE SIXTH SENSE

Rated: PG-13

Released August 6, 1999

Written by M. Night Shyamalan

Directed by M. Night Shyamalan

Distributed by Buena Vista Pictures

Starring:

Bruce Willis (Dr. Malcolm Crowe)

Haley Joe Osment (Cole Sear)

Toni Collette (Lynn Sear)

Olivia Williams (Anna Crowe)

Donnie Wahlberg (Vincent Grey)

Peter Anthony Tambakis (Darren)

Mischa Barton (Kyra Collins)

HAUNTED BY THE TRUTH

Cole Sear is not like other children. Terrifying visitations from the spirits of those who are not at rest have driven him into a state of debilitating anxiety. Enter Dr. Malcolm Crowe, a child psychologist who is dealing with "ghosts" of his own. Skeptical at first, Crowe's initial diagnosis that Cole is hallucinating dissolves into belief that he may be telling the truth about his eerie gift, especially when Crowe hears the spooky voices from the netherworld on a tape from his sessions with the boy.

As Cole's trust in his doctor grows, the frightened child agrees to respond to the ghosts to see if there is something he can do to bring them peace. One such specter is a girl named Kyra, who leads Cole and Crowe to discover she was actually the victim of foul play that now threatens her remaining sibling. With new confidence, Cole ventures to share messages from his grandmother that make his mother a believer and bring healing to her heart. Finally, Cole goes to work on Crowe's issues, urging him to speak to his wife about their own unfinished business by talking to her while she sleeps. In the end, Cole and Crowe part company, both having successfully "dealt with their stuff."

While many of us grew up to the motto, "There are no ghosts," Scripture has more to say than that. First, the Law of Moses forbade God's people to contact the dead by any means (see Deuteronomy 18:10–11). When King Saul went to the Witch of Endor to contact Samuel (see 1 Samuel 28), the departed prophet showed up, but he was none too pleased that Saul would seek wisdom in this way rather than by inquiring of the Lord.

In New Testament times, people still had some belief in ghosts, as we see from the disciples' reaction when Jesus approached them on the Sea of Galilee (see Matthew 14:26).

Further, after His resurrection, Jesus ate some fish to prove He was truly alive and not just an apparition. He had descended into Hades, preached to the captives there, conquered death, and been raised to life in a glorified, incorruptible body. His resurrection shows us we are destined for more than a disembodied afterlife or endless reincarnations. There truly is life (real life) after death at the final resurrection. As we fix our minds on these truths, we find freedom from fear and live today to the fullest.

*Just as we are now like the earthly man [Adam],
we will someday be like the heavenly man [Christ].*
1 CORINTHIANS 15:49 NLT

TAKE TWO

Do you harbor a secret fear of the supernatural, the unexplained, or the unknown? Take a moment right now and ask God to help you deal with that fear.

If you were to die tomorrow, what sort of "unfinished business" would you leave behind? What can you do to resolve those issues or situations today?

I've seen this movie ❏

My Star Review ☆ ☆ ☆ ☆ ☆

THE SOUND of MUSIC

Rated: G

Released March 2, 1965

Written by Ernest Lehman

Based on the Broadway musical: songs by Richard Rogers and Oscar Hammerstein II; musical book written by Howard Lindsay and Russel Crouse

Based on the book *The Story of the Trapp Family Singers* by Maria von Trapp

Directed by Robert Wise

Distributed by 20th Century Fox

Starring:

Julie Andrews (Maria)

Christopher Plummer (Captain Georg von Trapp)

Eleanor Parker (Baroness Elsa Schräder)

Richard Haydn (Max Detweiler)

Peggy Wood (Mother Abbess)

Charmian Carr (Liesl)

Heather Menzies (Louisa)

Nicholas Hammond (Friedrich)

Duane Chase (Kurt)

Angela Cartwright (Brigitta)

Debbie Turner (Marta)

Kym Karath (Gretl)

"FIND YOUR DREAM"

This heartwarming movie is set in 1938 Salzburg, Austria, just before the *Anschluss*—when the Nazis marched into Austria, forcing it to unite with Germany. Captain von Trapp, a retired naval captain and a widower, is oblivious to the emotional needs of his mischievous seven children, and runs his house in strict, military fashion. Realizing that his children need a mother, he prepares to leave for Vienna to court Baroness Elsa Schräder, and asks the Nonnberg Abbey to send him a temporary governess.

The fun-loving, carefree, and spontaneous Sister Maria simply isn't fitting in as a nun, so Mother Abbess sends her to the von Trapp home. Once there, Maria leads the children on frolics through Salzburg and the countryside, teaching them to sing, and when the captain and baroness return a month later, he is shocked by the change. Soon, however, he appreciates what Maria has done for his children, and during the baroness's visit, the captain and Maria realize they are in love.

Maria, embarrassed, flees to the abbey, insisting she is ready to take her vows to become a nun, but Mother Abbess wisely observes, "You have to live the life you were born to live," and sings a stirring song inspiring Maria to "follow ev'ry rainbow till you find your dream." Maria therefore returns and marries the captain. When they return from their honeymoon, however, the *Anschluss* has happened, and Captain von Trapp is ordered to join the German navy. Like Maria, the captain must follow his heart and make a difficult decision. He hates Nazism, so, forsaking his villa, lands, and worldly wealth, he leads his family across the Alps to freedom in Switzerland.

This movie has inspired millions to find their dreams, but warns that doing so comes at a price: We must often forsake material possessions, security, and comfort. As Christians, we realize that living the life we were born for, finding "our dream," means seeking God's plan for our life. Jesus promised great rewards and joy to those who follow Him, but also warned that becoming His disciple means forsaking much. (See Matthew 16:24–27; Luke 14:33.)

We bring difficulties upon ourselves when we seek God's plan for our lives, but it is worth the price we pay.

There is no man that hath left house, or brethren. . .
or lands, for my sake, and the gospel's, but he shall
receive an hundredfold now in this time. . .
and in the world to come eternal life.
MARK 10:29–30 KJV

 **TAKE TWO**

What dreams, if any, have you given up to be secure
financially? What can you do to begin working
toward God's vision for your life?

What difficulties have you encountered in seeking
God's plan for your life? What got you through those
trials? How can you help others realize their dreams?

I've seen this movie ❑

My Star Review ☆ ☆ ☆ ☆ ☆

Rated: PG-13

Released May 3, 2002

Written by David Koepp and Alvin Sargent (uncredited)

Based upon the comic book series *The Amazing Spiderman* by Stan Lee and Steve Ditko

Directed by Sam Raimi

Distributed by Sony/Columbia

Starring:

Tobey Maguire (Peter Parker/Spider-Man)

Kirsten Dunst (Mary Jane Watson)

Willem Dafoe (Norman Osborn/Green Goblin)

James Franco (Harry Osborn)

Cliff Robertson (Ben Parker)

Rosemary Harris (May Parker)

J. K. Simmons (J. Jonah Jameson)

Joe Manganiello (Flash Thompson)

"WITH GREAT POWER COMES GREAT RESPONSIBILITY"

Peter Parker, an orphaned teenager living with his aunt May and his uncle Ben, is the ultimate nerd—intelligent, skinny, and shy. He is hopelessly in love with a beautiful classmate, MJ (Mary Jane Watson), but he knows he can't compete with Flash Thompson, MJ's athletic boyfriend.

Then, while visiting a science display at Columbia University, Peter is bitten by a genetically altered spider. The next morning, he finds that his body is rippling with muscles and he has surprising new powers—so much so that he defeats Flash in a fight. But Flash, with his flashy new car, still wows Mary Jane, so Peter enters a wrestling match to win three thousand dollars in prize money, buy a car, and impress MJ.

Peter's uncle tells him that having the power to defeat the Flash Thompsons of this world isn't enough, but that "with great power comes great responsibility"—he must use his power unselfishly. Peter rejects his uncle's advice, but after he wins the wrestling match, instead of giving him three thousand dollars in prize money, the promoter gives Peter only a hundred dollars. Peter is so upset that when the promoter is robbed moments later, he refuses to stop the thief.

Two things happen to change Peter: First, the escaped thief kills Peter's uncle, driving home Peter's responsibility to stand up to evil. Second, a super-villain arises—the Green Goblin—who terrorizes New York. The Goblin invites Spiderman to join him, but Spidey refuses and risks his life to rescue others and to defeat the evil villain. As Peter later says, "Whatever life holds in store for me, I will never forget these words: 'With great power comes great responsibility.' "

Samson in the Bible had superhuman powers, as well. At first, like Spiderman, Samson looked out only for himself, lived selfishly, and used his powers to pulverize his enemies in personal feuds (see Judges 14:18–15:8).

Although we probably don't have outstanding powers, we, too, are often tempted to use our abilities and influence to aggrandize ourselves, win favor, and put others down. We know it's wrong, but it often takes a wake-up call for us to truly realize this. The Bible tells us instead that "we who are strong" should care for the weak "and not to please ourselves" (Romans 15:1 RSV).

*Do nothing from selfish ambition or conceit, but in
humility regard others as better than yourselves.
Let each of you look not to your own interests,
but to the interests of others.*
PHILIPPIANS 2:3–4 RSV

TAKE TWO

Do you live your life to glorify God or yourself? If the
latter, how can you turn this situation around so that
you are receiving praise for God rather than yourself?

Do you find yourself manipulating people or
situations to feed your own desires? How can
you make yourself more conscious—moment to
moment—of your motives?

I've seen this movie ❏

My Star Review ☆ ☆ ☆ ☆ ☆

Rated: PG

Released May 25, 1977

Written and directed by George Lucas

Distributed by 20th Century Fox

Starring:

Mark Hamill (Luke Skywalker)

Harrison Ford (Han Solo)

Carrie Fisher (Princess Leia Organa)

Peter Cushing (Grand Moff Tarkin)

Alec Guiness (Ben Obi-Wan Kenobi)

Anthony Daniels (C-3PO)

Peter Mayhew (Chewbacca)

David Prowse (Darth Vader)

James Earl Jones (Darth Vader's voice)

THE TRUE FORCE

"The Force," the impersonal universal power of the 1977 sci-fi classic *Star Wars*, is certainly not a God like we serve. But for purposes of the film, the Force serves as a kind of god, providing a reason for being and special powers for times of crisis. Obi-Wan explains the Force as "what gives a Jedi his power. It's an energy field created by all living things. It surrounds us and penetrates us. It binds the galaxy together."

Even the baddest of bad guys, Darth Vader, believes in the Force—though he draws his power from its "dark side." From the Death Star, the almost-operational secret weapon of the galactic Empire, Vader contemplates the danger of an attack from a ragtag rebellion led by Princess Leia, Obi-Wan Kenobi, and Luke Skywalker. The princess, it seems, has obtained the technical readings of the great space station, and sent them to the rebels via a small robot, R2–D2.

When Admiral Motti calls the Death Star "the ultimate power in the universe" and suggests obliterating a planet in a show of the Empire's might, Vader warns him of placing too much trust in technology. The Force, Vader insists, is a much more significant power.

Motti responds with irritation, mocking Vader's "sorcerous ways" and "sad devotion to that ancient religion." The Force, the admiral complains, hasn't produced the missing data tapes or helped Vader find the rebel's secret headquarters.

Wordlessly, Vader raises his hand, bringing his black-gloved thumb and fingers together in a pinching motion. Several feet away, physically untouched by Vader, Motti begins to choke, grabbing his neck in a futile attempt to break the mysterious stranglehold.

"I find your lack of faith disturbing," Vader growls.

It's a classic line from a classic movie—and it points, negatively at least, to a truth the *real* Force wants us all to understand: "Without faith it is impossible to please God, because anyone who comes to him must believe that he exists and that he rewards those who earnestly seek him" (Hebrews 11:6 NIV).

We live in a physical world but serve a spiritual God. We are finite, created beings; He is the infinite Creator. We perceive Him through the world we see around us, the Word He's given us, and the moving of His Spirit in our lives. And we take all of those things by faith.

*Jesus appeared to the Eleven as they were eating;
he rebuked them for their lack of faith and their
stubborn refusal to believe those who had seen
him after he had risen.*

MARK 16:14 NIV

 **TAKE TWO**

Do you have more faith in technology and material
things than in God? What can you do to escape the
stranglehold of "things" and return to the basics of
belief?

What can you do to help others realize a true Force
does exist? Perhaps inviting them to watch *Star Wars*,
then discussing it later, would pave the way to their
knowing a truly stellar God.

I've seen this movie ❑

My Star Review ☆ ☆ ☆ ☆ ☆

SUPERMAN
RETURNS

Rated: PG-13
Released June 28, 2006
Written by Michael Dougherty and Dan Harris
Based on a story by Bryan Singer, Michael
    Dougherty, and Dan Harris
Directed by Bryan Singer

Starring:

Brandon Routh (Clark Kent/Kel-El/Superman)
Kate Bosworth (Lois Lane)
Kevin Spacey (Lex Luthor)
James Marsden (Richard White)
Parker Posey (Kitty Kowalski)
Frank Langella (Perry White)
Sam Huntington (Jimmy Olsen)
Eva Marie Saint (Martha Kent)
Marlon Brando (Jor-El)

A SUPER SAVIOR LIGHTING THE WAY

Superman Returns begins five years after Superman mysteriously disappeared from Earth, searching in vain for Krypton, which he believed may not have exploded after his birth. Finding nothing more than fragments floating in space, he returns to Earth, only to discover crime is rampant and terrorists operate with impunity knowing the Man of Steel is no longer around to stop them. Worst of all, Lois Lane is engaged. She also has a young son (whose parentage is uncertain) and is the proud author of the Pulitzer Prize–winning article "Why the World Doesn't Need Superman."

After a brief visit to his adoptive mother, Ma Kent, Kal-El resumes his dual life as Clark Kent, gets his old job at the *Daily Planet*, and attempts to get reacquainted with Lois. But she has a big chip on her shoulder due to Superman's abrupt disappearance. So it's anything but a happy reunion. There's also the matter of her son's paternity to sort out.

While Superman is working through these tricky

personal issues, Lex Luthor—who's out of prison because Superman wasn't around to testify at his appeal hearing—steals Kryptonite from Superman's Fortress of Solitude and uses it to create an entire island that will wipe out North America, potentially killing hundreds of millions of people.

Once Superman learns of Lex's plans, he and Lois must set aside their personal problems so he can deal with the crisis. Racing against time, Superman has no choice but to literally sacrifice himself to save Earth. It's a climactic scene clearly meant to mimic the crucifixion. Like Jesus, Superman falls into the jaws of death when Luthor stabs him with a knife made of Kryptonite. But also like Jesus, he rises again to fight another day. In the end, Superman manages to thwart Luthor's evil plans and finally finds the home for which he's been searching—Earth.

Contrary to Lois's Pulitzer-winning article, *Superman Returns* makes a strong case for the biblical truth that without a savior, we are literally doomed. Romans 6:23 tells us, "For the wages of sin is death, but the gift of God is eternal life in Christ Jesus our Lord" (NIV). We all deserve to die for our rebellion against God. But in His grace, God did not give up on us. Like Jor-El, he saw that we "can be a great people. . .[we] wish to be. [We] only lack the light to show the way." Like Superman, Jesus came to Earth to show us the way, and the world has never lacked for light ever since.

*"I am the light of the world. Whoever follows
me will never walk in darkness, but will have
the light of life."*
JOHN 8:12 NIV

 **TAKE TWO**

Many people in the world today are like Lois,
questioning their need for a savior. If you were to
encounter such a person, what would you say?

What area of your life do you need Christ's light to
shine on today?

I've seen this movie ❑

My Star Review ☆ ☆ ☆ ☆ ☆

TITANIC

Rated: PG-13

Released December 19, 1997

Written and directed by James Cameron

Distributed by Paramount Pictures

Starring:

Leonardo DiCaprio (Jack Dawson)

Kate Winslet (Rose DeWitt Bukater)

Billy Zane (Caledon "Cal" Hockley)

Kathy Bates (Molly Brown)

Frances Fisher (Ruth DeWitt Bukater)

Bill Paxton (Brock Lovett)

CROSSING THE GREAT DIVIDE

This retelling of the 1912 sinking of the *Titanic* ze-roes in on a steamy fictional romance between Rose, an upper-class teenager, and Jack, a brash, handsome drifter, who won his berth in third class during a poker game.

Rose and her mother board the ship, along with Rose's controlling fiancé, Cal, whose wealth and power promise to bail the ladies out of ruinous debt. But Rose, unhappy with the arrangement, would rather end her life in the Atlantic. Jack saves her at the last moment, and she saves him from accusations of assault. A unique bond is born.

Strict class distinctions provide an impossible bar-rier for Rose and Jack's romance. But as the two still manage to get to know each other better, we become familiar with Cal's engagement gift, a necklace called the "Heart of the Ocean," which becomes Hockley's excuse to frame Jack for theft, winding the latter up in the brig. When the ship strikes the fateful iceberg, Rose braves the chaos of fleeing passengers and incoming saltwater to release Jack. But they both end up overboard in the icy waves where only one of the pair manages to fit on a piece of floating wreckage, the other slipping into the cold, dark depths forever.

Although the film glorifies a sexual tryst outside of traditional Christian mores, it also critiques the obvious folly and injustice of artificial boundaries such as the class system of that day, showing them to be ridiculous and hypocritical, especially since Rose gives the appearance of aristocracy when her financial state is far worse than Jack's. One can also see the bondage of classism in the necessity of Rose's marriage to someone she doesn't love just to maintain her family's social standing.

This critique of the artificially binding walls of race, class, gender, and age is central to the New Covenant. Jesus broke every wall of partition between Jews and Gentiles, slaves and free people, men and women. The Spirit is poured out on all flesh regardless of gender, age, or wealth (see Acts 2:17–18).

It is alarming how worldly categories continue to cling to human culture—worse still when we encounter them in the Church. By God's Spirit, let us take up the challenge of applying the gospel message wherever we catch a scent of their subtle presence in our midst.

My brothers, as believers in our glorious Lord Jesus Christ, don't show favortism.... If you show special attention to the man wearing fine clothes and say, "Here's a good seat for you," but say to the poor man, "You stand there" or "Sit on the floor by my feet," have you not discriminated among yourselves and become judges with evil thoughts?
JAMES 2:1, 3–4 NIV

 **TAKE TWO**

What sorts of class or racial barriers exist in your community? What can you and/or your church do to lead the way in breaking them down?

Examine your own thoughts, conversations, and attitudes lately. Do you catch a "whiff" of any of the structural prisons mentioned above? If so, take a moment to seek God's forgiveness and ask Him to help change your attitudes and future behavior.

I've seen this movie ❑

My Star Review ☆ ☆ ☆ ☆ ☆

To Kill a Mockingbird

Rated: Unrated

Released December 25, 1962

Written by Horton Foote

Based on a novel by Harper Lee

Directed by Robert Mulligan

Distributed by Universal Pictures

Starring:

Gregory Peck (Atticus Finch)

John Megna (Charles "Dill" Harris)

Phillip Alford (Jeremy "Jem" Finch)

Mary Badham (Jean Louise "Scout" Finch)

Brock Peters (Tom Robinson)

Collin Wilcox (Mayella Ewell)

Robert Duvall (Arthur "Boo" Radley)

James Anderson (Robert "Bob" Ewell)

THE TRIALS OF PREJUDICE

This story is set during the Great Depression in the town of Maycomb, Alabama, where six-year-old tomboy Scout Finch and her older brother Jem live with their widowed father, an attorney named Atticus Finch. Life is normal in this "tired and sleepy town" until the day that a black man, Tom Robinson, is accused of raping a white woman, Mayella Ewell, and the court appoints Atticus as Tom's lawyer.

Tom faces such hostility from the townsfolk that Atticus must defend him from a lynch mob. During the court case Atticus proves that Mayella and her father, Bob Ewell, are lying, and in his closing argument, Atticus gives an impassioned plea for the jury to find Tom innocent. The jury follows its prejudices, however, and declares Tom guilty. While Atticus prepares to appeal the verdict, Tom tries to escape prison and is shot dead. The children's faith in the justice system is shattered. Yet their respect for their father, who stood against prejudice, has grown as, after the verdict, Atticus turns to leave, the blacks in the courtroom balcony rise, and Reverend Sykes says to

Scout, "Jean Louise, stand up. Your father's passing."

Yet the children, too, are guilty of prejudging people. A shut-in named Boo Radley has been the talk of the town for years and many people think he's insane. Jem describes Boo as a monster. Yet after the trial, Bob Ewell, furious about being exposed, attacks Scout and Jem when they're walking home in the dark, and it is the mentally challenged Boo who comes out of hiding to defend them, then carry the injured Scout home.

Deeply held opinions can affect our judgment, causing us to prejudge a person or situation. We can also make mistakes if we leap to conclusions before we hear all the facts. In the early days of Israel, the tribes living in Canaan became furious when they heard the Israelites east of the Jordan River had built an unauthorized altar. They marched out to wage war on them, and only when they learned the stone altar was simply intended as a memorial did they sheath their swords. (See Joshua 22.)

Proverbs 18:13 cautions, "He who answers [or judges] a matter before he hears it, it is folly and shame to him" (NKJV). Or as Atticus tells Scout, "If you just learn a single trick, Scout, you'll get along a lot better with all kinds of folks. You never really understand a person until you consider things from his point of view. . . . Until you climb inside of his skin and walk around in it." Let's take the time to consider others' points of view.

*"Do not judge according to appearance,
but judge with righteous judgment."*
JOHN 7:24 NKJV

 **TAKE TWO**

Have you ever prejudged someone? Did you
feel ashamed afterward? How can you prevent
prejudging in the future?

Have you ever been ostracized for defending a victim
of prejudice? Was it difficult being ridiculed for your
stance?

I've seen this movie ❏

My Star Review ☆ ☆ ☆ ☆ ☆

TOY
STORY

Rated: G

Released November 22, 1995

Written by Joss Whedon, Andrew Stanton, Joel
  Cohen, and Alec Sokolow

Story by John Lasseter, Peter Docter, Andrew
  Stanton, and Joe Ranft

Directed by John Lasseter

Distributed by Walt Disney Pictures

Starring (voices):

Tom Hanks (Woody)

Tim Allen (Buzz Lightyear)

John Morris (Andy Davis)

Erik von Detten (Sid Phillips)

Don Rickles (Mr. Potato Head)

Jim Varney (Slinky Dog)

Annie Potts (Bo Peep)

Wallace Shawn (Rex)

ENVY IN ACTION

In this hilarious animated movie, Woody is an old-fashioned cowboy doll and, as Andy's favorite toy, the respected sheriff and leader of all the other toys. One day, just before Andy's family moves across town, Andy receives a new action figure for his birthday—the Space Ranger Buzz Lightyear of Star Command.

Buzz has so many cool features that all the other toys stand in awe of him—and he quickly displaces Woody as Andy's favorite toy. Woody laments, "What chance does a toy like me have against a Buzz Lightyear action figure?" To complicate matters, Buzz cannot accept that he is a mere toy, but thinks he is an actual space ranger on a mission to save the galaxy.

Woody, overcome with envy, states, "You stay away from Andy. He's mine, and no one is taking him away from me." Woody decides to replace Buzz on a family outing by pushing him down behind Andy's desk, but things go wrong when Buzz accidentally falls out the window instead. The other toys turn against Woody, believing he tried to murder Buzz.

Woody realizes he must rescue Buzz, and the adventure that follows is a hilarious lesson on the consequences of envy. Woody attempts to convince Buzz that he is a mere action figure and Buzz finally accepts the fact. For his part, Woody finally admits that Buzz is a lot cooler than him. In the end, each toy risks his life to rescue the other—and wind up reunited with all the other toys at Andy's new house.

In the Bible, Jacob had a favorite son, Joseph, and gave him a beautiful multicolored robe. Joseph's ten older brothers were so envious of Joseph that they sold him as a slave into Egypt, then told their father that Joseph had been killed by a wild beast (see Genesis 37). We may think that *we'd* never do something so heinous out of envy, but remember, Woody wasn't trying to kill Buzz, either.

The Bible warns that "wrath killeth the foolish man, and envy slayeth the silly one" (Job 5:2 KJV), and points out that "where envying and strife is" the door is open to "*every* evil work" (James 3:16 KJV, emphasis added)—including things we thought we'd never do. So don't allow yourself to envy.

*But if ye have bitter envying and strife in your hearts,
glory not. . . . For where envying and strife is,
there is confusion and every evil work.*
JAMES 3:14, 16 KJV

TAKE TWO

Have you ever been jealous of someone or something? Did it bring out the worst in you? How can you prevent the green monster from stealing your joy (and that of others) in the future?

Do you play favorites—at home, work, school, or church? Does doing so open the door to strife? What can you do to rectify the situation?

I've seen this movie ❑

My Star Review ☆ ☆ ☆ ☆ ☆

WALL-E

Rated: G

Released June 27, 2008

Written by Andrew Stanton and Jim Reardon

Original story by Andrew Stanton and Peter
  Docter

Directed by Andrew Stanton

Distributed by Walt Disney Pictures

Starring (voices):

Ben Burtt (Wall-E and M-O)

Elissa Knight (EVE)

Jeff Garlin (Captain McCrea)

Fred Willard (Shelby Forthright and BnL CEO)

MacInTalk (AUTO)

John Ratzenberger (John)

A MAJOR RECLAMATION PROJECT

WALL-E is the sole robot left to clean up Earth seven hundred years after humans abandoned it because mountains of trash left the planet uninhabitable. At first, the humans, now living on the space ship *Axiom*, hoped to return once the garbage was dealt with but, concluding the toxic environment cannot sustain life, the interstellar cruise ships send out probes in search of other homes.

After centuries of isolation, WALL-E is confronted by EVE, a "female" probe who is on a quest for life forms. Immediately smitten, WALL-E hitches a ride on her ship when she returns to her base with a plant that shows there may be hope for Earth after all. Aboard the ship, we see how humanity has "evolved." Soft and overweight, our descendants can't even stand up on their own. They live virtual lives through gizmos from the comfort of levitating lounge chairs.

With EVE's discovery, the ship's captain realizes his people must return to Earth and start afresh, but AUTO, the ship's mutinous autopilot, disagrees. Our heroes must fight to overcome him with the destiny of Earth's people hanging in the balance.

It's only natural to compare WALL-E with the story of Noah and the ark (Genesis 6–8). In both cases, the world as we know it has been destroyed because of humankind's rampant irresponsibility. The survivors of this disaster are set adrift in an unimaginably vast sea of watery waves/star systems, the natural consequences of self-indulgence. EVE, like Noah's dove, searches for a little plant as evidence of a place to land the respective "arks." Both stories use great global disasters as a canvas on which to paint a redemptive new beginning. The animated images of our future during the closing credits were the most significant of the film as we see the rise of the new earth and the transformation of the people who rebuild it (see Revelation 21–22).

This pattern of rise-rebellion-judgment-restoration, repeated throughout the Bible, points to the need for a global Deliverer. With the coming of Christ, the groundwork for God's kingdom and the template for the "new humanity" have been established. History is heading toward one grand redemption—the marriage of heaven and earth under the governance of our Prince of Peace (see Isaiah 9:6–7).

*Then I saw a new heaven and a new earth, for the
first heaven and the first earth had passed away. . . .
I saw the Holy City, the new Jerusalem, coming
down out of heaven from God, prepared as a bride
beautifully dressed for her husband.*
REVELATION 21:1–2 NIV

 **TAKE TWO**

WALL-E embarks on a quest for love that ultimately
redeems humanity. In what ways does his journey
parallel Christ's journey? In what way is it different?

In *WALL-E*, humans have become their own worst
enemies, the victims of their own vices and selfish
desires. What do you think this film is saying about
the fate of humanity? What hope does it offer for
"salvation"?

I've seen this movie ❏

My Star Review ☆ ☆ ☆ ☆ ☆

THE WIZARD OF OZ

Rated: PG

Released August 25, 1939

Written by Noel Langley, Florence Ryerson, Edgar Allen Woolf

Based on the novel by L. Frank Baum

Directed by Victor Fleming; uncredited Richard Thorpe, George Cukor, and King Vidor

Distributed by Metro-Goldwyn-Mayer

Starring:

Judy Garland (Dorothy Gale)

Frank Morgan (Professor Marvel/the Wizard of Oz)

Ray Bolger (Hunk/the Scarecrow)

Bert Lahr (Zeke/the Cowardly Lion)

Jack Haley (Hickory/the Tin Man)

Billie Burke (Glinda)

Margaret Hamilton (Elmira Gulch/the Wicked Witch of the West)

UNVEILING THE TRUTH

The *Wizard of Oz* is an enjoyable classic and one of the best-loved movies of all time. The story follows Dorothy and her dog, Toto, as a tornado plunks them into a strange land called Oz. When her house accidentally lands on the Wicked Witch of the East, Dorothy is lauded by the locals—Munchkins—and granted magical ruby slippers that protect her from the vengeful Wicked Witch of the West. All Dorothy cares about, though, is getting home, so she is advised to seek help from the Wizard of Oz, who reigns from the Emerald City.

Along the way, she overcomes a series of perils with the help of the heartless Tin Man (who really is kind), the Cowardly Lion (who really is courageous), and the brainless Scarecrow (who is quite clever). After defeating the witch and exposing the wizard, Dorothy discovers her companions already possessed what they were seeking. Glinda, the Good Witch of the North, finally reveals that Dorothy can return home, using the mantra, "There's no place like home," while clicking the heels of her red slippers.

On the surface, the movie suggests a straightfor-ward and entertaining conflict between good and evil. But the most telling scene—Toto's tearing away the veil to reveal the fraudulent Great and Powerful Oz—suggests something more. Toto is probably the true hero of the story, for this unveiling is exactly what the great spokesmen—from Elijah to John of Patmos to Martin Luther King Jr.—have always done. They con-fronted the powers, tore away veils of deception, and gave us an opportunity to see reality from heaven's perspective.

For example, like Toto, the book of Revelation tears back the imperial curtain to expose Almighty Rome the Savior of the World as Rome the Violent Beast, Rome the Whore, Rome the soon-to-be-vanquished Babylon. Conversely, John's visions show us the cru-cified Christ has not been defeated. He has actually triumphed over Satan, sin, and death, and now sits on heaven's throne. The persecuted and vanquished churches are reminded, "Things are not as they seem."

Personally, the prophets also allow us to look in the mirror to see who God sees rather than buying in to what marketers, accusers, or flatterers want us to see. In grace, Jesus sees the true image of God at the core of our hearts. He welcomes our true self—hearts, brains, and courage—to come forward on His path of discipleship, grander than any yellow brick road.

*Whenever anyone turns to the Lord,
the veil is taken away.*
2 CORINTHIANS 3:16 NIV

 **TAKE TWO**

God often "tears back the veil" to help us see the truth. When was the last time He did this for you? What lie clouded your ability to see? What truth did He reveal?

Like Toto, God has also called us to tear back the veil to allow others to see. Ask God to show you how you can do this for the people in your life.

I've seen this movie ❑

My Star Review ☆ ☆ ☆ ☆ ☆

 **AUTHOR INDEX**

ED STRAUSS

Home Alone: Standing in the Breach
Hoosiers: "More Than Conquerors"
The Incredible Hulk: Taming the Beast Within
Independence Day: Battling the Destroyer
Jaws: "Looking for Someone to Devour"
Jurassic Park: You Could—But Should You?
King Kong: Manipulating Monsters
Liar, Liar: "The Truth Shall Set You Free"
The Lion King: Claiming Your Rightful Place
The Lord of the Rings: The Fellowship of the Ring:
The Most Unlikely Imaginable
My Big Fat Greek Wedding: One Big Family
National Treasure: "You're Treasure Hunters, Aren't
   You?"
North by Northwest: A Case of Mistaken Identity
The Passion of the Christ: The Ultimate Sacrifice
The Princess Bride: "As You Wish"
Schindler's List: Saving Lives, One by One
The Shawshank Redemption: The Power of Hope
The Sound of Music: "Find Your Dream"
Spider-Man: "With Great Power Comes Great
   Responsibility"
To Kill a Mockingbird: The Trials of Prejudice
Toy Story: Envy in Action

KEVIN MILLER

A Beautiful Mind: The Courage of the Heart
Casablanca: "Here's Looking at You, Kid"
Charlie and the Chocolate Factory: "The Best Kind of Prize"
Dead Poets Society: Choosing Captains
Elf: Finding Yourself Has Never Been So Much Fun
Enchanted: Hope-Filled Romantic
Juno: Beyond Ourselves
Life Is Beautiful: Eyes on the Prize
Minority Report: "You Can Choose!"
Pirates of the Caribbean: The Curse of the Black Pearl: Where Do You Store Your Treasure?
Raiders of the Lost Ark: The Ultimate Quest
Rocky: Fight the Good Fight!
Shrek: Stuck in a Swamp
Signs: What Kind of Person Are You?
The Sixth Sense: Haunted by the Truth
Superman Returns: A Super Savior Lighting the Way
Titanic: Crossing the Great Divide
WALL-E: A Major Reclamation Project
The Wizard of Oz: Unveiling the Truth

PAUL MUCKLEY

Back to the Future: Don't Look Back
The Poseidon Adventure: Lifesaving 101
Star Wars: The True Force

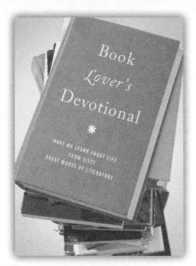